Additional praise for *How to Find a Job, Career and Life You Love*:

Louis' book is a little gem of a tool. It's for every person who has ever yearned to live their right and purposeful life, the one dreamt of but hasn't quite been put into action. As a human resources executive who has spent thirty years coaching, advising and helping people with their career aspirations, this book will be a tremendous kickstarter. Instead of plodding through the career that life has thrown at you, you can learn how to re-set, recalibrate what is truly important, meaningful and energizing and determine with intentionality the life and career you are meant to live. Bravo Louis on *How to Find a Job, Career and Life You Love*.

Lisa Peterson, senior practice expert at Gallup

How to Find a Job, Career and Life You Love was a game changer and a lifeline for me. By applying the practical tools that Louis provided, I was able to find out where and why I was losing my power and most importantly, how to get it back. After each chapter I was left with so many takeaways and clear guidance on where I was headed next. Louis is a visionary and a healer do not be fooled by his youthful appearance - he is full of wisdom beyond his years. Thank you Louis for rekindling the passion in me that I thought was forever lost - for this and for so much more I am forever grateful!

Linda Scull, RN

Louis is one of the rare break of leaders that can touch you emotionally and intellectually. *How to Find a Job, Career and Life You Love* will resonate with you because it makes sense rationally and reaches out to you personally.

Louis is a leader who brings his intuition and blends it with insight and facts to make you enthused to read more and begin acting!

Pat Beyer, senior medical device executive

Read this book only if you're ready to do some soul searching that results in real-life planning. Louis' book is a must for anyone who is willing to take action and live life with more purpose.

Greg Jordan, small business owner - Greg Jordan Design

The idea of work-life balance is eroding very quickly. We spend too much time at work for it to be anything other than deeply satisfying and meaningful. However, for most of us, none of our high school or college coursework was focused on finding meaning through our work. Louis' book is exactly what we should be teaching in high school and college. Louis presents a step-by-step guide for how to connect "who you are" with "what you do." If you are looking for a life of meaning, read this book immediately.

Brian Mohr, co-founder and managing partner of Y Scouts

HOW TO
FIND A JOB,
CAREER
AND LIFE
YOU LOVE

A journey to purpose, fulfillment and
life happiness

LouisEfron.com

DISCLAIMERS

How to Find a Job, Career and Life You Love is for educational and informational purposes only. Louis Efron, LLC makes no guarantees that you will achieve a better job, career, or life as a result with this book. Changing jobs, careers, and lifestyles have risk and not everyone will experience success. Making decisions based on any information in this book should be done only with the knowledge that you could experience significant loss, or find yourself in an even more undesirable situation in life. Use caution and seek advice of qualified professionals when attempting any life change.

Your level of success in attaining any result is dependent upon a number of factors including your skill, knowledge, ability, dedication, personality, work ethic, job and career goals and interests, focus, business savvy, job market, locality, and financial situation. Because these factors differ according to individuals, Louis Efron, LLC cannot guarantee your success in any job, career, or life.

You alone are responsible and accountable for your decisions, actions and results in life, and by your use of this book, you agree not to hold Louis Efron, LLC nor the author liable for any such decisions, actions or results, at any time, under any circumstances. You agree that Louis Efron, LLC and the author are not responsible for the success or failure of your job, career, or life decisions relating to any information presented in this book and you specifically release Louis Efron, LLC or any of its representatives or contractors and the author from liability for any special or consequential damages that result from the use of, or the inability to use, the information, questions, exercises, or strategies presented and communicated in this book and its materials and websites, or any services provided prior to or following this book, even if advised of the possibility of such damages.

ISBN 978-0-9960828-2-2
ISBN 978-0-9960828-3-9 (ebook)

Second Edition

THIS BOOK IS DESIGNED TO HELP YOU FIND PURPOSE,
FULFILLMENT AND MORE HAPPINESS IN LIFE BY
EXPLORING NEW PROFESSIONAL HORIZONS,
MAKING JOB AND CAREER DECISIONS FOR THE RIGHT
REASONS, AND LOOKING AT LIFE OPTIONS FROM A
DIFFERENT ANGLE.

WISHING YOU A BLESSED JOURNEY AND LIFE!

Whenever I pick up a book filled with "expert advice", my first question is, " . . . is this person truly an expert and is what they're telling me for real?" Well, with Louis Efron, it takes about a page and a half to be sure . . . he's not only the real deal, but his writing style is some of the most transparent, vulnerable, relevant and timely you'll ever read!

This book made me reevaluate my entire purpose for living and has had a profound impact on my work with corporate clients and how they can best optimize employee engagement. With his unique experience in theatre and human resources, Louis gets right down to the personal stuff and hits on what truly makes people want to do and be their best. The idea of combining Employee Purpose with Corporate Purpose is a great way to help people be everything they can be as human beings, but can't help to maximize ROI and improve culture . . . why didn't I think of this?

This book is not only a fascinating read, but is destined to be part of a new paradigm in corporate human resources strategy.

John Schaefer, founder and president of Schaefer Recognition Group

As the CEO of two successful recruitment firms, I know the importance of placing people in the right jobs to ensure their success and happiness. This process starts with candidates understanding their purpose: what they were put on Earth to do. Louis' book and process helps job candidates and employees find their purpose. It is suggested reading for everyone applying for positions through my firms. *How to Find a Job, Career and Life You Love* is a game changer for job seekers, employees and every organization.

Max Hansen, founder and CEO of Job Brokers and Y Scouts

FOR MY FATHER

TABLE OF CONTENTS

IMPROVING YOUR JOB AND CAREER

SETTING YOUR COURSE

TAKING THE FIRST STEP

ENSURING ALIGNMENT

EMBRACING YOUR FUTURE

TOOLS TO HELP YOU

BEHIND THE SCENES

Everything comes if a man will only wait. I've brought myself by long meditation to the conviction that a human being with a settled purpose must accomplish it, and that nothing can resist a will that will stake even existence for its fulfillment.

– Benjamin Disraeli

PLEASE NOTE:

Throughout this book I refer to both jobs and careers:

A *job*   is a focused activity or task.

A *career*   is an occupation over a significant period of time, most
             likely involving different jobs.

For example, a person with a 20-year *career* in finance may have held *jobs* as an accounts payable clerk, payroll administrator, credit manager, budget analyst, accounts receivable manager, accountant, comptroller or finance director.

*****

At the end of most chapters you will be prompted to answer thought-provoking questions in a Purpose Box looking like this one, along with rating answers to simple statements. Tallying answers to the rated statements will provide you with your Purpose Alignment Indicator Score™. This can be done when you complete the book or you may go to my website at LouisEfron. com to electronically verify your score in advance.

To fully engage in this book, document your answers and ratings.

In the TOOLS TO HELP YOU section of this book are templates (available free for download at LouisEfron.com) to help you accomplish this, along with additional questions to assist you in finding your purpose. It is recommended that you copy or download the Purpose Box Questions now for use during your reading of this book.

THANK YOU FOR ...

- **Your investment** in this book. If used fully, it will positively change your life.

- **Your time** is your life and your life is your time – there is nothing more valuable.

- **For believing** that you can actually earn a living doing what you love – I am doing it, and I know many others who are doing it, too.

- **Your commitment** to action – nothing will happen without it!

- **For giving me a chance** to let me help you live an even happier and more fulfilled life – **you deserve it!**

FOREWORD

People are always blaming their circumstances for what they are. I don't believe in circumstances. The people who get on in this world are the people who get up and look for the circumstances they want, and if they can't find them, make them.
– George Bernard Shaw, *Mrs. Warren's Profession*

Louis Efron is one of our brightest lights for illuminating key steps to living on path and on purpose.

Louis and I were brought together through a mutual friend on our paths of purpose. We share a deep passion for serving and helping others and a desire to fulfill our purpose in life. Our lives came together to support each other in these endeavors.

In my book *Aspire* I help people discover their purpose through the power of words including the deeper, sometimes hidden meanings. My own journey involved a fateful encounter with a Viennese shopkeeper who revealed a secret word to me which changed my mindset and set me on a quest to understand the words affecting our principles and our behavior. A renowned etymologist provided the mentoring I needed to achieve my goal of bringing value and meaning to other people's lives.

How to Find a Job, Career and Life You Love uses a practical approach similar to Stephen R. Covey's *The 7 Habits of Highly Effective People* where a paradigm shift or dramatic change is needed to realign your actions and behaviors along with the usage of positive thinking. The resulting transformation begins your journey towards a fulfilled and purpose-driven life.

In Louis' book, you will discover your purpose through targeted questions and exercises, real life examples, scientific studies and the use of tools like S.L.A.M. to modify your behaviors and streamline your life helping you focus on your end goal: a life fulfilling your purpose. Louis also lays out a process to target Your Next 30 Days+, plus provides a Purpose Master Action Plan™ to support your journey to living your life of purpose.

How to Find a Job, Career and Life You Love accompanies you on your pathway to living a meaningful life. First you will recognize how to live without regrets while you seek alignment with your purpose. You will analyze your situation and stay on track using S.L.A.M. A good portion of the book deals with improving your situation at work, or if necessary how to move on to a job better suited to your strengths and purpose, which may be at your current employer. As you set your course and proceed toward your goal you will encounter help from others. The book will also help you build confidence and to envision, embrace and ultimately design your future.

Use the book over the next month, by taking time to pause and reflect and to sleep on questions in your life at the end of chapters, as Louis advises. This allows your conscious and subconscious to become a proactive team with the end goal of following and fulfilling your purpose.

How to Find a Job, Career and Life You Love will enrich your life. I invite you to begin your proactive journey towards living a life you love now.

- Kevin Hall, author of *Aspire: Discovering Your Purpose Through the Power of Words*

INTRODUCTION

> If you change the way you look at
> things, the things you look at change.
> – Dr. Wayne Dyer

Finding a job, career and life you love isn't automatic. It takes commitment, unconventional thinking, honestly surveying your life from all angles and some risk, but it is possible. I spent decades searching for my purpose-filled professional and personal life. This book shares my successes, failures, learning and strategies so you, too, can live the life <u>you</u> want and are intended to live.

During my life I explored and experimented with my career and jobs to find my true path. I have been a: store clerk, holiday gift wrapper, salesman, installer, gym attendant, bellhop, designer, hair model, waiter, night shift supervisor, coffee shop manager, administrator, personal assistant, writer, stage manager, theatrical director, Broadway theatre manager and Off-Broadway producer, labor-relations specialist, human resources manager, global human resources and charity executive, contributor to *Forbes* and *Huffington Post* and entrepreneur.

There are many tools available to enhance your growth and success as you move towards a life of purpose. Some strategies described in this book you will use directly and others I will mention for additional study on your own. In any case, my hope is to shorten your learning curve so you will experience success quicker, benefitting from what I share with you and my years of experience.

In my corporate life, I successfully used the problem-solving method described by Edward de Bono in his 1985 international bestseller *Six Thinking Hats*. In de Bono's process, participants wear different colored hats to represent distinct modes of thinking. White stands for facts, yellow for the positive, black for the negative, red for the emotional and green for new ideas. The meeting facilitator wears a blue hat.

Six Thinking Hats is successful because it provides a practical and positive approach to making decisions and exploring new ideas. The technique helps the wearer focus and think in unexpected and creative ways about the challenges he or she are facing – looking at all sides of a problem. It promotes reasoning that is counterintuitive and thinking that doesn't spring from traditional step-by-step logic. It stimulates the kind of thinking that everyone needs to successfully manage their personal and professional life.

Another tool I use for approaching problems and questions unconventionally is more common than hats: sleep. Remember, the unconscious mind is a powerful tool. You can use its' benefits as I do, by thinking about challenges – creative, business, personal – right before bed. I usually wake up with my answers. Sometimes I recollect a solution that appeared in a dream. Other mornings, I wake up with a big "a-ha!" Sleeping allows my brain to attack problems from different directions.

Dr. Joanne Cantor's book *Conquering Cyber Overload* cites research that proves "let me sleep on it" is an effective way to find better solutions. Cantor's book explains, at certain phases of sleep your brain becomes even more active if you've just learned something new. Sleeping helps clarify what you've just learned. Finally, it sets "the stage for the emergence of insight." The unconscious mind is a powerful tool.

In my book, both distinct modes of thinking and sleep play a role in promoting 360-degree thinking.

At the end of most chapters in *How to Find a Job, Career and Life You Love*, I ask you to "PAUSE NOW and reflect" to answer questions or rate statements. These statements may be followed by additional exercises. This structure will help you look at and think about your job, career and life situation from different angles. I recommend you make an effort to answer each chapter's questions just prior to going to sleep.

Early in my career a wonderful mentor of mine encouraged me to take time each day to think and reflect. He told me this time would help me better focus on the things that truly mattered. Once I did this, I found I made better decisions in my job and life, plus I moved from being reactive to proactive. The simple act of pausing for five minutes to think and reflect on a problem, challenge, or consider my day, changed my life. And it will do the same for you.

Whether in your office, at home, in the shower, on a run, walk, or bike ride, the time you spend thinking and reflecting will pay huge dividends. To maximize this benefit, take Dr. Joanne Cantor's advice and "sleep on it." I will remind you to do so throughout this book.

Chapter questions or statements should be read and then honestly, thoughtfully and thoroughly answered in writing. Before going to sleep, re-read the questions and your responses. For this to be effective, try to get seven to nine hours of sleep. It's also important not to distract your mind with any other content – like reading, television, music, email, or conversation between rereading the questions and your answers and going to sleep.

To further assist you in your 360-degree thinking, I provided additional purpose-based questions broken down into thinking themes in the back of this book under Supplemental Purpose Questions. I highly recommend you review these questions and think about, answer, then sleep on the ones relevant to you and your situation.

Chapter statements requiring a 1 through 5 rating (1 being "Strongly Disagree" and 5 being "Strongly Agree") will be used at the conclusion of this book to calculate your Purpose Alignment Indicator Score™. Your score can also be obtained electronically by completing the Purpose Alignment Indicator Survey™ on my website at LouisEfron.com.

You can also revise or add questions relevant to your situation or choose from the additional Supplemental Purpose Questions.

Your personal, emotional and intellectual connection to all your responses are critical to the success of this process. If you don't hold your responses in your heart and mind, you won't be true to yourself and will not find the job, career and life alignment you want, need and deserve.

The true power of this book requires you document all your answers/ratings then lay them side-by-side for comparison, re-evaluation, analysis and potential revision before finalizing and actioning your Purpose Master Action Plan™ (a.k.a. your Purpose

M.A.P.™). The Purpose M.A.P.™ is a tool to help guide your successful, purpose-driven future. It will be discussed in a chapter at the end of this book. Creating your Purpose M.A.P.™ may require you to return to previous chapter sections to readdress your answers, ratings, decisions, solutions and sleep on them further.

The US Army slogan "Be all that you can be" drove recruitment success for over twenty years. *How to Find a Job, Career and Life You Love* is designed to help you see, plan and implement a truly self-actualized future – a better way forward and a happy, purpose-driven life with no regrets. Changing who you are - or pretending to be someone else - does not deliver greatness and fulfillment in life; but changing how you think and behave makes the difference between despair and a life of happiness, success and purpose.

Enjoy your journey to the job, career and life you want, need and deserve!

- Louis Efron

GETTING
STARTED

Chapter 1

YOUR PURPOSE IN LIFE

> If you want to lift yourself up,
> lift up someone else.
> – Booker T. Washington

My purpose is to enlighten, inspire, and teach . . . to help others see the possibilities in life.

I began as a five-year-old designing a pen with a light on it so my far-sighted grandmother could read her favorite book. In my recent corporate life, I worked as a human resources professional always focused on helping others.

Helping people grow and succeed is what I spend my time thinking about, what keeps me awake at night, and what gets me up in the morning. There is nothing more fulfilling or emotionally charging for me than watching others win. It is my reward for what I do. It is my purpose. Their smiles lift my spirits and make me feel good about life. When I find myself doing things unaligned with my purpose, I make an effort to do them less or, if possible, not at all.

The Merriam-Webster Dictionary defines purpose as: "the reason for which something is done or used: the aim or intention of something." I prefer the Purpose Institute's more focused definition of purpose: "a definitive statement about the difference that you are trying to make in the world." Please keep the latter definition in mind as you read through this book, answer the questions, do the exercises and contemplate your own purpose.

I believe whether you work for yourself or someone else, you should feel an equal amount of job and life engagement.

Living a life of purpose means doing things with a deep, personal meaning to you, regardless of how - or even if - you get paid for them. Through effort, you can achieve this goal. When you do, you will not be able to distinguish the line between work and play and will find that the resources you need to sustain yourself and your family will flow into your life in abundance.

PAUSE NOW and reflect:

What do I believe to be my purpose in life (i.e., my definitive statement about the difference I am trying to make in the world)?

Please rate the statement below:

I am confident about my purpose in life.

Strongly Disagree 1 2 3 4 5 *Strongly Agree*

Remember to sleep on it.

Don't despair if you are having trouble responding to the above question and statement. These are big and important topics to consider. Take your time. You will get another chance to respond to them at the end of this book.

Remember to record your answers to the questions and the ratings. The more time that passes the less likely you will recall the information. Writing down your answers will allow you to review and revise them later, as needed. You may use the templates in the TOOLS TO HELP YOU section of this book to assist you with this.

Chapter 2

EXTRA TIME ON EARTH

> The past is a ghost, the future a dream. All we ever have is now.
> – Bill Cosby

I recently stumbled across Bronnie Ware's article "Top 5 Regrets of the Dying." Bronnie, a writer and singer/songwriter from Australia, spent several years caring for dying people in their homes. When she began asking the people she cared for about their regrets in life, she received deep insights, shedding light on what is truly important. Their top regrets included:

1. I wish that I had let myself be happier.

2. I wish I'd had the courage to live a life true to myself, not the life others expected of me.

3. I wish I didn't work so hard.

4. I wish I'd had the courage to express my feelings.

5. I wish I had stayed in touch with my friends.

A friend of mine lost her mother shortly after college following several years battling cancer. During the struggle, her mother expressed regrets about how she lived her life, especially regrets about the courage to live her own life and express her feelings. Given more time after her first bout with cancer, my friend's mother used what she called her "extra time on Earth" to remedy some of those regrets.

Despite trying to value her extra time on Earth, during her last months in hospice care my friend's mother brought up things she would never achieve in life and how she would miss out on her children's future. My friend took her mother's experience to heart. She values each day and lives it with courage instead of fear.

Throughout this book I will touch on most of the five regrets listed above and give you alternatives so you can live a life without regrets.

At the end of the classic book *The Death of Ivan Ilych* by Leo Tolstoy, the character Ivan questions his life before dying. Despite his outward success, he wondered if he lived it all wrong.

Success in life is about asking the right questions at the right time . . . not at the end of your life or tomorrow, but today, before it's too late. Don't postpone your life waiting for the right time to live. That time may never come. We all have stories of people who waited to make a reconciliation call, tell someone they loved them, take their dream vacation, visit a friend or relative, or try something they always wanted to, but never got the chance to experience. My Depression era grandparents never enjoyed several rooms in their own home because they didn't want to ruin the furniture. It is pointless not to live your life today while you can.

This book is filled with the right questions. Ask and answer them now, action your responses, and you can embrace your extra time on Earth.

PAUSE NOW and reflect:

If today were my last day, I would regret . . .

Regrets can be emotionally charged. Write down your responses, then write an action plan below each regret, explaining how you will transform your regrets into accomplishments. Keep the document somewhere you can see it and track it daily. This is a hard task and one most people don't achieve. Unless your plan is visible daily, it will soon be forgotten and only remembered when it may be too late.

Please rate the statement below:

I have no regrets in life.

Strongly Disagree 1 2 3 4 5 *Strongly Agree*

Remember to sleep on it.

Chapter 3

ONE LIFE TO LIVE

> The two most important days in
> your life are the day you are born
> and the day you find out why.
> – Mark Twain

Do you ever awake in the morning and ask yourself, am I:

- in the right job?

- at the right organization?

- on the right career path?

- doing what I am supposed to be doing with my life?

- happy and fulfilled?

You are not alone.

I left a profession I loved to chase money. Then I left an amazing company after eleven years for even more money. I found myself at the wrong company, in the wrong place in life and had to course correct.

A recent Gallup study concluded that 87% of workers worldwide are not engaged at their jobs. And Deloitte's Shift Index survey indicated that 80% of workers don't like their jobs. The average worker in America works 8.8 hours a day, but the study numbers suggest very few of those workers jump out of bed every morning excited to go to work.

With only one life to live, why are so many people struggling to be happier in life? They are not asking the right questions.

I aim to help you ask yourself the right questions with this book. The rest is up to you. Why waste your efforts, money and time when you can earn more, do more and be more by implementing the changes you discover here?

As Amelia Earhart noted of her courageous and purpose-driven life, "The most difficult thing is the decision to act, the rest is merely tenacity."

Today is your day. It is yours to live. Seize the moment. Find a job, career, and life you love now.

Transform your responses below into action.

PAUSE NOW and reflect:

Am I in the right job, career and organization? If not, why?

Please rate the statement below:

I am doing what I am supposed to be doing with my life.

Strongly Disagree 1 2 3 4 5 *Strongly Agree*

Remember to sleep on it.

Chapter 4

LIVING YOUR PURPOSE

> When you are inspired by some great purpose, some extraordinary project, all your thoughts break their bounds. Your mind transcends limitations, your consciousness expands in every direction and you find yourself in a new, great and wonderful world. Dormant forces, faculties and talents become alive, and you discover yourself to be a greater person by far than you ever dreamed yourself to be.
>
> – Patanjali

The other day I was asked to do a presentation for my daughter's kindergarten class about the illustrator John James Audubon. Having never heard of him, I typed his name into Google and was delighted to discover an amazing man with an inspirational story of purpose.

Audubon was born on April 26, 1785. He was a French-American ornithologist, naturalist and painter known for his detailed illustrations documenting a wide array of American birds in their natural habitats. During his lifetime he identified twenty-five new species of birds. Without strong belief in his life purpose, Audubon would not have succeeded as one of the greatest ornithologists of all time.

His family had other plans. Audubon's father was a sea captain and wealthy businessman. He urged his son to follow the same path, but the younger Audubon wanted to draw birds. From his earliest days birds held sway over him. "I felt an intimacy with them," he once explained, ". . . bordering on frenzy [that] must accompany my steps through life."

At age twelve, Audubon was sent to military school and then became a cabin boy. Seasickness along with dislike of math and navigation plagued him. Audubon failed the officer's qualification test, officially burying his father's hopes for a naval career.

Once again, Audubon returned to the woods, often collecting bird nests and eggs to sketch. Over the early years, Audubon struggled financially. Regardless, he stayed the course he loved and felt he was good at – his purpose – to study, draw and educate the world on his beloved birds.

Audubon's major work, a color-plate book entitled *The Birds of America* (1827–1839), earned him legions of admirers, including scientists and European royalty. After spending much of his early life avoiding his father's attempts to make him a respectable businessman, Audubon achieved world recognition by selling his drawings of birds.

Today, a single engraving - earning Audubon $2.00 in his lifetime - sells for $50,000.00. A complete set of his drawings is valued at about $2,000,000.00.

Audubon spent the last nine years of his life with his wife Lucy on their thirty-five acres of property facing the Hudson River (in what is now upper Manhattan). He died in 1851 at age sixty-five after living a transparent life of purpose.

PAUSE NOW and reflect:

What was I most fascinated with as a child?

Please rate the statement below:

My younger self would enjoy what I am doing now in life.

Strongly Disagree 1 2 3 4 5 *Strongly Agree*

Remember to sleep on it.

Chapter 5

MY JOURNEY

> Our plans miscarry because they have no aim.
> When a man does not know what harbor he is
> making for, no wind is the right wind.
> – Seneca (4 B.C. – 65 A.D.)

Back in 2000, I found myself staring at the two small, silver loop earrings in my left earlobe. I was in a hotel room at a five-star beach resort in Puerto Rico with my then-girlfriend. For the first time in almost 10 years, I contemplated taking my earrings out for good.

How had I reached this point?

I graduated from California State University, Fullerton with a degree in Theatre Arts. Immediately I moved from California to New York to pursue my dream of becoming a New York City theatre artist.

After a brief stint as a bellhop, then a night shift supervisor at a conference center outside of Manhattan, I landed the job that launched my dream career in the arts: a producing associate position with a successful Broadway producer and general manager paying $250.00 a week. This job led me towards independent producing and directing, plus other work with the New York City Opera.

I remember thinking at the time, "If I can make $500.00 a week, I will be golden." During my five years producing, managing, directing and writing theatre I received some favorable reviews and made a small amount of money. But I had to wait tables to make up the difference between my salary and expenses. I loved moving from one theatre production to another, but did not enjoy moving from my own apartment to a rented room to lower my rent costs. I wanted and needed more stability in my life.

I needed a steady job. I found one at the union, representing theatre actors.

From my office at the union I looked out over Times Square and saw the various theatres where I previously worked. Three years later, I found myself negotiating a $2,000.00 increase on an employment offer for a senior labor rep position in Chicago. I thought the job was mine. But I lost it to someone who, unlike me, accepted the union's original, lower offer.

My experiences flashed through my mind as I stared into the mirror at those little earrings. My luxurious surroundings had intoxicated me. It sickened me to realize I scraped together every dime to make a romantic two-day getaway possible. I wanted a better life for my girlfriend and me. As I contemplated where I stood in life, I realized working at a union wasn't fulfilling the goals I set when I moved to New York. I decided if I must spend my days doing something other than personally creating art, I should make a reasonable living doing it.

It was time to leave the arts to chase money in corporate America.

I knew I had to reinvent myself to attract a large employer. To accomplish this I needed to be methodical and strategic in my approach. I added distance-learning law degrees (a BS and JD) to complement my theatre degree and union experience, thereby increasing my value as a labor specialist.

My earrings came out and my career, job and new life lessons began.

II

<u>PAUSE NOW</u> and reflect:

Have I missed any critical road signs or clues about the direction I was traveling in life? If so, why did I miss them?

Please rate the statement below:

I am happy with my life's story.

Strongly Disagree 1 2 3 4 5 *Strongly Agree*

Remember to sleep on it.

Chapter 6

YOUR DEFINITION OF SUCCESS

> It is never too late to be what
> you might have been.
> – George Eliot

My father was a great man. After graduating from Brooklyn College with a degree in mathematics, he began his career as a programmer at IBM and worked his way up into the executive suite. By retirement age, my father had registered numerous patents in multiple industries. He won a technical Academy Award for the computerized film printing process he developed.

Despite his corporate success, my dad loved the theatre. He became a kid in a candy shop when performing in front of an audience. He spent a good portion of his youth performing and working in theatre, including a short stint with the Long Beach Civic Light Opera in California.

As a young boy, my siblings and I accompanied our father and mother to a theatre production every few months. Without fail, my father ushered us to the stage door to meet the cast after the performance ended. This interaction with spirited actors further fueled my love of theatre.

If my father cultivated any thoughts of becoming a full-time theatre performer himself, those dreams would have been quickly squashed by his working class father. My grandfather spent his life selling hats for a living. Getting a job at a good company, working hard and becoming an executive epitomized his definition of success. Even though my own father encouraged my childhood love for the arts, his personal success in corporate America subtly defined what I came to consider as success for me, too. Had my father chosen an artistic path in life, I might never have left my career in theatre.

PAUSE NOW and reflect:

What is _my_ definition of success?

Please rate the statement below:

I am living _my_ definition of success.

Strongly Disagree 1 2 3 4 5 _Strongly Agree_

Remember to sleep on it.

Chapter 7

SEEK ALIGNMENT

> Happiness is not something
> readymade. It comes from your
> own actions.
> – Dalai Lama

I have always been interested in connecting with and helping others. As a child I wanted to help my maternal grandfather at his plumbing and heating business. While in New York City, I chose to direct theatre productions I knew would move my audience. I sought out roles in human resources and in organizations helping others live more fulfilling lives. Today, I donate my time to charity in an effort to save the lives of children with cancer and to build schools for children in need of educational facilities.

In everything I do, connecting with and helping others is always my focus. This living a life of purpose didn't happen by accident. I made it happen. You can, too.

My successes occurred because I made a conscious effort to understand my innate talents. I developed and trained those talents, transforming them into strengths. I then chose employment to match my passions and interests. Ensuring your natural talents, core passions and interests are in sync with your career is vital to success, fulfillment and happiness in much of life. When any component is misaligned, it is impossible to realize your true potential and accomplish all you were put on Earth to do.

Several years ago, I had the pleasure of working with a certified R&D rock star. His teams created an endless string of top-selling products. The company recognized promise in their golden boy. They put him through a top executive MBA program, eventually promoting him to president of the organization. Within six months he found himself on the outs with just about everyone in the organization. After a long and mostly brilliant career, he lost his job.

After recovering from the shock of what had happened, a competitor quickly picked up the failed president. Soon he led successful product development teams again.

The company that released him made a common, but major error. It relocated a talented person, but placed him in a position where he could no longer use his natural talents. His employer wanted to use his long record of success within its broader business, but that meant playing him out of position. He produced top-selling products by inspiring his engineers, but was unable to engage the rest of the organization in the same way, most notably the global sales force. His remarkable failure at the first company is a good example of what happens to anyone who disregards what they are naturally good at in life or who is placed in a role at odds with their innate talents.

This problem is not unique to the corporate world. It extends across all human endeavors.

In 1993, Michael Jordan left the Chicago Bulls to play for a minor league baseball farm team in Birmingham, Alabama. He brought his ferocious work ethic to the sport, but baseball just didn't align with his talents.

He was a mediocre baseball player. In the spring of 1995 he returned to basketball and continued his unparalleled career.

Despite the obvious importance of aligning a job seeker's abilities with his or her job, a 2012 Gallup study indicated that only 50% of U.S. workers use their strengths throughout their day. Employees at large organizations might be more effective when placed in a different position at the same organization.

How often are you doing what you do best in your current position? When looking for a job and career you love it is important to know, understand, and maximize your passions, talents and strengths. Next ensure you are in a role where you can leverage them most of the time. You are certain to increase your job engagement, productivity and happiness. Your employer may even appreciate your efforts more.

From the first formal recognition I received as a ten-year-old short story writer to my commercial success with *Forbes* and *Huffington Post* three decades later, I slowly developed confidence in my writing skills. My natural talents became strengths. I gained the exposure needed to feed my core passion and interests. Soon, I connected with more people than I ever dreamed possible.

The Clifton StrengthsFinder® remains one of the best assessment tools I have come across to uncover talents. I highly recommend using their online process to gain a better understanding of what you do best. The profile I received early in my career played a large part in guiding decisions in my life and the successes that followed those decisions. More details on this can be found under Additional Resources in the TOOLS TO HELP YOU section of this book.

(II)

PAUSE NOW and reflect:

What am I most passionate about?

Please rate the statement below:

I spend most my time on things that leverage my passions, talents and strengths.

Strongly Disagree 1 2 3 4 5 *Strongly Agree*

Remember to sleep on it.

Chapter 8

YOUR GOALS

> Build your own dreams, or someone
> else will hire you to build theirs.
> – Farrah Gray

A few years ago, Dr. Gerald Bell, a professor at the University of North Carolina in Chapel Hill published a study where he asked 4,000 retired executives – whose average age was seventy – one question:

If you could live your life over again, what would you do differently?

The number one response:

I should have taken charge of my life and set my goals earlier. Life isn't practice; it's the real thing.

While I thought I had taken charge of my life at thirty-two, I had set all the wrong goals. I never asked myself what I ultimately wanted in life, what I wanted to be remembered for and what I wanted to leave behind in the world.

For most people, setting goals is more difficult than achieving them. Figuring where you are going is usually harder than getting there.

As a runner, I always train better when I set the time and distance for my upcoming run. I track my running speed and distance with a phone app. I know how fast I am running, how far I have travelled, and how much faster and further I must go to reach my goal. When I can see a finish point (a stop sign, traffic light, landmark, finish line), I find myself running faster despite how tired I am or how far I have already run. This same phenomenon occurs in other runners keeping up with or passing me in the final stretch of a race. The moment I look down at the ground or away from my goal, I start to feel myself slowing down. There is a strong urge to give into my fatigue. To effectively achieve goals, they must be clear and visible. If you can't understand and see your goals, they will be difficult - if not impossible - to achieve.

My friend and author, Kevin Hall, recently introduced me to a life-changing way to develop, focus on, and achieve goals – the vision board. A vision board is a place to capture your goals and dreams. It can be made of almost anything – corkboard, cardboard, paper, foam core, wood or glass. The concept is to attach pictures, magazine clippings, words, or things representing your goals. It must be big enough and displayed where you are likely to see it each day. Imperative goals are placed in the center and others of lesser importance spread out towards the edges. Remember, everything on your vision board should be significant goals to you and ones you want to achieve - despite how challenging you may perceive them to be.

Once these goals are in front of you daily – in your home, office, bedroom, bathroom - they are real and become achievable. If you begin to doubt something you want is achievable, think about the fact that men first stepped on the moon with less sophisticated technology than most digital watches use today. Or recognize there are athletes who won Olympic gold medals missing limbs or being unable to walk.

Focus and believe . . . "And will you succeed? Yes! You will, indeed! (98 and ¾ percent guaranteed)!" – Dr. Seuss. *Oh, The Places You'll Go!*

⏸

PAUSE NOW and reflect:

What do I want to be remembered for in life? Can I <u>see</u> that goal?

Create your vision board now.

Write a list of the goals you want to achieve. Number them in importance ("1" being most important on down to the least important). Now attach text or visual representations of your goals to your Vision Board placing the most important in the center surrounded by other goals important to you.

Please rate the statement below:

If today were my last day, I fulfilled my purpose in life.

Strongly Disagree 1 2 3 4 5 *Strongly Agree*

Remember to sleep on it.

ANALYZING
YOUR
PRESENT
SITUATION

Chapter 9

FINDING YOU

> The only person you are destined to become is the person you decide to be.
> – Ralph Waldo Emerson

The first step in my search for a new career involved creating a resume to rebrand my past experiences. I wanted my resume to fit the corporate job I desired and felt I could get: labor-relations specialist. My resume transformed from a list of my Broadway and other theatrical productions to a detailed description of my interactions with unions, plus my people and financial management experience. To ensure I got it right, I enlisted a professional resume writer to help recast the last eight years of my life.

With my new resume in hand, I set a goal: apply for six labor relations jobs on Monster.com every night. In less than two weeks, I got the call that would change my life. The head of a Chicago-based recruitment firm contacted me to discuss an opportunity at a large medical device company as a labor relations specialist in one of their New Jersey manufacturing plants.

After a barrage of phone and in-person interviews, I hit a home run and landed the job, doubling the salary I earned at the union.

Even though I did not have "me" fully figured out, I was able to accomplish my goal of obtaining a good job at a great company. A new chapter in my journey had begun.

PAUSE NOW and reflect:

How accurately does my resume reflect what I am most passionate about? How can I reflect this even stronger?

Please rate the statement below:

My resume best reflects who I am and what I really want.

Strongly Disagree 1 2 3 4 5 *Strongly Agree*

Remember to sleep on it.

Chapter 10

GETTING BACK ON PURPOSE - S.L.A.M.

> I am not a product of my circumstances.
> I am a product of my decisions.
> – Stephen R. Covey

With so many options and pressures in life, it is easy to get sidetracked and spend your time on the wrong things. Whenever I drift from my purpose in life or stray from my course, I ask the following four questions to **S.L.A.M.** myself back onto my intended path:

What do I need to **Subtract** from my life?

What do I need to do **Less** of?

What do I need to **Add** to my life?

What do I need to do **More** of?

I ask these questions of myself and write down my responses before I go to bed, allowing my subconscious mind to ponder my thoughts. When I wake-up, I make any needed revisions and then commit to my intended actions. These four questions always bring me back on track. Doing this helps me recognize what is truly important.

A recent **S.L.A.M.** of mine looked like this:

I will **subtract** from my life: negative self-talk and worrying about things I can't control.

I will do **less** of: answering non-essential emails and interrupting time with my family for business tasks that can wait.

I will **add** to my life: monthly catch-up calls with extended family and friends, plus daily dedicated "me time" to think and unwind.

I will do **more**: date nights with my wife and fundraising for charity causes important to me.

What do you need to **S.L.A.M.** in your life?

By asking the four questions above on a regular basis and following through on any course corrections, you will be able to stay on purpose, experience personal greatness, fulfillment and happiness, plus make your intended mark on the world. By using **S.L.A.M.** regularly, you will ensure you live your life deliberately and on purpose.

Be proactive. Don't allow others to make these important choices for you. Keep your intended actions to no more than two per question and make them actionable immediately. You can go back and add more actions to your list later as your life changes. Commit to your changes once the need is before you.

PAUSE NOW and reflect:

What do I need to **Subtract** from my life?

What do I need to do **Less** of?

What do I need to **Add** to my life?

What do I need to do **More** of?

Please rate the statement below:

I frequently check to make sure I am on the right path in life and course correct when needed.

Strongly Disagree 1 2 3 4 5 *Strongly Agree*

Remember to sleep on it.

Chapter 11

BEYOND MONEY

> Certain things catch your eye,
> but pursue only those that
> capture the heart.
> – American Indian Proverb

Money hasn't been around long in the scheme of human existence, but it quickly became our ultimate distraction. The first question most job seekers ask a potential employer is "How much does the position pay?" While most of us need money to survive, the answer to this question should never be the key driver to move things forward.

As a purpose coach, the first question I ask my clients is: "If you didn't need money, what would you do in life?" While most of us can't eliminate money from the question of where and why we work, this is a great theoretical question to probe your inner desires. The answer can help you discover your life purpose.

What about taking action in the income-driven reality most of us face?

In her book, *Get a Life, Not a Job: Do What You Love and Let Your Talents Work For You*, Dr. Paula Caligiuri offers a suggestion. By actively seeking multiple streams of income, you can achieve the freedom to follow what you love and not be financially beholden to a job you don't. This can be in the form of a home-based business, speaking on your topics of expertise, teaching others about something you love, investing, or even taking a second job doing what you love.

Begin with an Internet search for someone currently working in the career or position you desire. LinkedIn is an excellent resource for this. Review their work accomplishments and skills, contact them for advice. Don't feel you need to reinvent the wheel; emulate what you can and start making it happen. With the advanced, accessible and low-to-zero cost technology available today, there are no excuses for not using these tools to assist you in achieving the situation you want and need.

To help me start my home-based business, I attended Brendon Burchard's six-week online Total Product Blueprint workshop, his live workshop of the same name and his live four-day Experts Academy event. All gave me the information, tools and resources I needed to get my side business (now full-time) off the ground. You will read a bit more about Brendon later in this book. I have also provided his website details in Additional Resources in the TOOLS TO HELP YOU section.

PAUSE NOW and reflect:

If I didn't need money, what would I do in life?

Please rate the statement below:

I would want to perform my job even if I didn't get paid for it.

Strongly Disagree 1 2 3 4 5 *Strongly Agree*

Remember to sleep on it.

Chapter 12

AVOIDING BAD MARRIAGES AND BAD JOBS

> When couples break-up, arguing that their partner does not know them, the exact opposite is true: They know them – they simply do not like them.
> – Anonymous

Unfortunately, I know about bad marriages. My first was a disaster. It lasted only about three weeks, but took three years to escape. We fell in love with the idea of romance, ignoring the major red flags along the way. We met online, felt the magic, got engaged a few weeks later, spent most of the following months planning an elaborate wedding, married one year from our first date and were both speaking to lawyers about three weeks after that. We spent a year focusing on wedding details instead of getting to know each other.

I'm not alone in my mistakes. When searching for life partners, many people end up with fantasies instead of real people. One result of this tendency is the 50% divorce rate for first marriages in the US. But our predisposition for idealizing others doesn't end with finding potential partners. We romanticize all sorts of things - the past, childhood, foreign places, our grandmother's cooking, the lifestyles of celebrities and . . . jobs. The result: 80% of workers want to divorce their jobs.

The parallels between bad marriages and unhappy jobs develop at the beginning. When people search for jobs, they scan the web for attractive companies that grab their immediate attention. They look at an organization's career page for openings, read the job descriptions, then redraft their resume and pitch it to fit the role they think they want. They recreate themselves to another's specifications.

From the outside, we can easily see how this could end badly. The organization is pitching its most attractive side – whether real or perceived – and the candidate is tailoring the perception of who he or she is to meet the needs of the organization. Six months down the road both sides are unhappy. Some of these relationships limp along for years producing minimal value. Others end abruptly, causing disruption and financial strain for both parties.

Years ago, an actress I asked out had these choice words for me: "I know you think you like me, but *men are often taken by me based* on the characters I am playing. In truth, *you don't know me* aND THEREFORE IT Would *be impossible* for you to like me." My only regret looking back now was that I did not heed her warning before diving into my first marriage.

PAUSE NOW and reflect:

What are the attributes of a job and career I would love?

Please rate the statement below:

I have thoughtfully designed my life.

Strongly Disagree 1 2 3 4 5 Strongly Agree

Remember to sleep on it.

IMPROVING YOUR
JOB AND CAREER

Chapter 13

SEEK A POSITIVE CHANGE

> Life is 10% what happens to you
> and 90% how you react to it.
> – Charles Swindoll

As a theatre director I always coached my actors never to make a move on stage to get away from something, but rather to move towards something - to make a positive choice. This same principle applies to your job and career. If you don't feel you are adding value in your current job or at your organization, you won't jump out of bed each morning and deliver your full potential.

Start looking for that connection either in your current organization, in a different job, or at another organization performing in the same job function. When you identify your target, make the move to acquire it.

Transitions take time. Please do not be discouraged by this.

In the meantime, develop the skills which will help you fulfill your purpose. Momentum can energize you. Take a class, develop a hobby or find a mentor in your new career. Seek out like-minded professionals at group events to either get involved or stay involved in your interests.

Even small changes can make a world of difference in your life. A college friend of mine knows pain first-hand for she experiences it daily with Fibromyalgia. Walking through the grocery store was problematic for her over a decade ago. Instead of giving into the pain when first diagnosed and allowing it to dominate her life she found small, positive solutions to reach her larger goal. For a week she walked to the corner every day. The next week she walked a little further. Eventually she walked three miles at a time. She moved towards the new life she wanted without fighting to regain what she lost.

You don't need to change jobs to find happiness, if you feel you are adding value to your organization and those around you. When working conditions are not quite right, it is worth talking to your manager or Human Resources professional for resolution before quitting your job.

However, no matter how great everything else is in your current job, if you can't see the value you bring to your organization, you will never be truly happy or engaged in your work. At that point, move to a better place for the sake of everyone — most importantly you.

PAUSE NOW and reflect:

What positive changes can I make in my job to improve my current situation?

Please rate the statement below:

I am making positive choices in my life.

Strongly Disagree 1 2 3 4 5 *Strongly Agree*

Remember to sleep on it.

Chapter 14

WHEN TO SPEAK TO YOUR BOSS

> Strive not to be a success,
> but rather to be of value.
> – Albert Einstein

Reaching out to your boss should be your first step when you feel disconnected to the mission and purpose of your organization. Part of a manager's duty is to help guide and engage the employees reporting to them. If he or she can't explain and help you understand how your work adds value to your organization's overall objectives, you should seek an answer elsewhere in the organization. If no one can connect the dots for you, then it may be time for a job or organization change.

A friend of mine in the Northwest helped grow a company from small to significant. Her position grew with the company, but she could never seem to get the additional help she needed. After years of working 70+ hours a week she broke down in tears, lamenting it was time for a big change.

The more she thought about her situation, the more she realized how much she loved the company and how important its mission and purpose was to her. She decided to present the facts to her boss on why she needed help again. This time she acquired the resources she needed.

Had she not possessed the courage to ask for help, the company would have lost a valuable person and she would have left a job she really loved.

Research has consistently shown that a lack of job connection to an organization's mission and purpose significantly impacts employee engagement. If your current employer can't help you make that connection, it's time for a change.

In any case, remember that moving on isn't the same as moving forward.

PAUSE NOW and reflect:

Have I spoken to someone who can help me solve challenges in my life and job which I can't solve myself? If not, why?

Please rate the statement below:

I always ask for help when I need it.

Strongly Disagree 1 2 3 4 5 *Strongly Agree*

Remember to sleep on it.

Chapter 15

WHEN TO STAY

> When I let go of what I am,
> I become what I might be.
> – Lao Tzu

While I was incredibly excited about my new adventure and the money I would make as a labor relations specialist, in the back of my mind I hoped to return to being a theatre artist within a few years. My idea was to incorporate into my art my new corporate perspective on how to make money.

Almost exactly six months into my new job I found myself again sending out resumes to find an even higher paying job. I had been placed under a newly hired manager who lacked fundamental people skills. My engagement began to drop quickly. I later realized I was fortunate enough to not have any takers. Not only was my new manager let go after three months, but I began to further connect to the purpose of the organization. The division president started bringing in patients helped by the products the company produced to share their life stories with employees.

Both events re-engaged me. I no longer reported to a difficult manager and the stories of the patients really touched my heart and personal purpose. It affected other employees at the organization deeply, too. Whether putting small beads on the surface of a knee implant or working in sales or human resources, after hearing how someone's life had been saved or improved by your personal contribution – no matter how small – we felt part of something bigger than just a job.

Now I wanted to stay. I was engaged in the organization's mission and purpose. It felt good.

PAUSE NOW and reflect:

Do I feel part of my organization's mission and purpose?

Please rate the statement below:

I am engaged in my organization's (or own business') mission and purpose.

Strongly Disagree 1 2 3 4 5 *Strongly Agree*

Remember to sleep on it.

Chapter 16

WHEN TO MOVE ON

> How wonderful it is that nobody
> need wait a single moment before
> starting to improve the world.
> – Anne Frank

If you are working, polling numbers strongly suggest you would like a different job. But if you realize you are unhappy with your job, you shouldn't necessarily sprint for the doors. This book is designed to help facilitate change, but the transformations must <u>be positive</u> and <u>fit your goals</u>. I don't want to encourage you to become one of those people who manically and without direction pursue happiness without really knowing what they want. Ironically, this quest for happiness leaves many people upset or worried they will never enjoy work or life unless they choose the perfect career.

But it's not that simple — or that desperate. In his *New York Times* bestseller *Great Work*, David Sturt asserts most of the fulfillment we experience comes, not from finding that one-in-a-million position, but from making a difference in the job we already possess.

For me, David's comment about making a difference is the key to most employee engagement issues. No matter where they live or who they are people need to feel they are <u>adding value to something bigger than themselves</u>. If they don't feel this, a lack of self-worth will quickly lead to depression and disengagement.

In Dan Ariely's TED talk, "What makes us feel good about our work?" he describes several experiments in which people were paid to do a simple task with decreasing amounts of compensation.

The groups were divided into three categories:

- those that had their work *acknowledged*

- those that had their work *ignored*

- those that had their work *destroyed* after completion

In all the experiments, participants regarded work that was ignored in the same regard as work that was destroyed.

Additionally, those that felt their work had no meaning or offered no value were more likely to produce lower quality work or to cheat, regardless of the compensation being made. Those that had their work acknowledged did more work for less compensation, at a higher quality and with a greater level of care. The basic human need to feel their work mattered made a massive impact on both how engaged they were in their jobs and the results they delivered.

If you speak to any motivational speaker or self-help guru, they will tell you that self-worth - knowing you matter - must come before you can truly care for anything else in life. Not surprising, this also applies to the workplace.

To solve our job-engagement problem, each and every employee must ask himself or herself one question:

Am I adding value in my job?

If the answer is no, do something about it. Reposition yourself in your current role (1 will teach you how to do this in the next chapter, Adding More Value to Your Current Organization), move to a different position within your organization, or if these prove impossible, look for a new employer – maybe even working for yourself.

PAUSE NOW and reflect:

What specific things can I do today to add more value to those around me?

Please rate the statement below:

I am adding value in my job, career and community.

Strongly Disagree 1 2 3 4 5 *Strongly Agree*

Remember to sleep on it.

Chapter 17

ADDING MORE VALUE TO YOUR CURRENT ORGANIZATION

> Eighty percent of success is showing up.
> – Woody Allen

My new division president peered out of the window as I entered the building. This was his daily routine to ensure his employees put in a full day's work. His division was doing very well, but not because of the president's timekeeping. Its success came from employees who believed in the purpose of the organization and delivered results. Because he never figured out what drove his unit's success, the president's days of standing by the window were numbered. He was replaced by a leader who understood how to engage purpose-driven employees.

At another organization I visited, employees made sure they were sitting behind a cluttered desk when the president walked by. They had learnt that an empty and organized office set off alarm bells that they weren't working.

The above practices are signs of immature leadership and limited organizational potential. But they are also fairly common. Most people have spent some time in a role where they had to deal with bosses who demanded attendance over outcomes and theatrical busywork. For some people, nothing is more attractive than a job requiring so little. Don't be late, leave a little bit after quitting time, don't take excessively long lunches, use sick days only when you are sick – and never put your feet up on the desk. Barring any major performance issues or downsizing, you are likely to have a job until retirement.

However, if you want more out of your career and aspire to deliver real value to your organization and those you serve, you will have to take things beyond the 80% that Woody Allen speaks about in the above quote.

To truly add value to your organization and those around you, you must be in a position where you can do what you do best - most of the time - and you must be able to quantify your results. Doing this will allow you to get noticed, receive promotions, make more money, and feel good about your contributions.

For commercial businesses, this means figuring out how your job, and what you do, connects to serving your organization's customers, selling more products and doing business for less. For not-for-profit organizations, you must show how your job, and what you do, adds value to the mission of the organization and any fundraising efforts.

In 1993, you would have found me working as a bellhop in Tarrytown, New York. I was pretty good at my job and did fairly well on tips. However, about 50% of my job caused me a lot of pain: driving guests to destinations around town. On one such occasion, I was called upon to drive a group of Japanese businessmen who had just flown in from Tokyo to a meeting. The meeting was only five miles away. This should have been a short, easy trip. However, my poor sense of direction made it feel like the distance of the plane journey the businessmen had just been on. My three non-English speaking passengers were now running late for the meeting they had flown 6,700 miles to attend. I was seriously lost and had to stop for directions. All I could hear was what sounded like, "We are going to kill you!" being shouted from the backseat by the culturally punctual businessmen.

It's funny now. At the time I wanted to run from the car and keep going.

My 20% told me if I treated these businessmen extremely well and got them to their meeting on time, I would increase the chance they and their company would return to the conference center adding to the sales, profits, growth, sustainability, good word of mouth and success of my employer. Not to mention a possible tip for me. However, I did not have the natural talent (a sense of direction) to deliver on my 20% and failed miserably despite my best intentions.

To deliver optimum value for your organization, you must be in a role that plays to your strengths.

To connect your job to the results your organization is looking for, ask yourself four questions:

1. What is my organization's purpose (why does it exist)?

2. How does my daily work connect to my organization's purpose?

3. How do I make (or raise) money for my organization?

4. How do I help control costs for my organization?

The answers to these questions will highlight the reasons your organization invested in you and what they want in return for that investment.

Now ask the question that adds the maximum value for you and your organization:

How does my purpose support the purpose of my organization?

The answer to this question creates the magic alignment where all great things happen. This is where both employee and company know they were put on this earth for the same reason. Combined with being in a role that plays to your strengths, nothing is more powerful to drive performance, results and success than the extra 20%.

PAUSE NOW and reflect:

How does my purpose support the purpose of my organization? If it does not, how can I create this alignment in my life?

Remember to sleep on it.

Chapter 18

LEAVING A GOOD THING

> Twenty years from now you will
> be more disappointed by the
> things that you didn't do than
> by the ones you did do.
> – Attributed to Mark Twain

Despite my sense of adventure only eleven years earlier, 2011 found me in a different place as I re-examined my career path. The thought of exploring other job opportunities terrified me. I had a high paying job at a really great company with superior benefits, a wife and one young daughter with plans for a second child. I also had a large mortgage and lots of expenses. Speaking to people about their past jobs and those who left my current company for other opportunities, I knew the grass wasn't always greener.

Fearing a failed move, I didn't look for another job. Instead, I decided to make an attempt at some side businesses to explore an alternative career that might put me on a path of greater purpose and fulfillment. Despite attempts at businesses from management consulting to children's illustrated book publishing to private equity development, I struggled to find fulfillment in my side ventures and ultimately dropped them.

Then an executive headhunter contacted me with another option. The recruiter sent me a message on LinkedIn asking if "I knew anyone" who might be interested in a VP of international human resources role at a software company based near my home in Scottsdale, AZ. The role offered a chance to increase my compensation and move my wife and daughter back to their native UK for a while.

It was also an opportunity to experience a new industry and career challenge, which fed the learner in me. I did know someone and it was me!

Shortly after starting the new role, I realized I might have made a big mistake. The company culture was not a fit for me. Also, despite the success I had in my role internationally, I had no plans to retire at the organization. When my international work wound down I was offered to head up global recruiting for the company. At that point I led with my heart and parted ways with the organization.

I followed the lead of a friend who left a corporate VP position to pursue a better life alignment. After some trial and error with various types of jobs, he found career happiness in an unlikely position: as a café manager. He decided he didn't like the stress of the corporate world, was really good with people and liked interacting with them throughout his day. He loved food and serving others and wanted to spend more time with his family within a structured life. He was able to check all his boxes, find a job he loved – despite a significant reduction in pay – and started living the life he desired.

PAUSE NOW and reflect:

What would I most miss if I left my current organization? Can these things be replaced elsewhere?

Please rate the statement below:

I have the life I want.

Strongly Disagree 1 2 3 4 5 *Strongly Agree*

Remember to sleep on it.

Chapter 19

THE MYTH OF HARD WORK

> You want to work really, really,
> really hard? You know what?
> You will succeed . . . the world will
> give you the opportunity to work
> really, really, really hard.
> – Larry Smith,
> *Why You Will Fail to Have a Great Career*

"Work hard, my boy and you will be successful," was my paternal grandfather's childhood advice to me.

Even though he had been dead for many years, his words never stopped ringing in my head. I decided to take his advice again when entering the corporate world, commit myself to a good job, then work as hard as I could to build a successful career. It worked!

Not long after accepting my first corporate role, I was promoted to the human resources manager for the manufacturing site where I had been hired. I did not know it at the time, but this would be the beginning of a career roller coaster that never entered even my wildest imagination.

Six months later, I was told that the company was consolidating their division's five-plant manufacturing system down to four. My site would close. While it was a very sad and emotional time for everyone working at the facility, it turned out to be a monumental learning experience for me.

After successfully leading the manufacturing site closure for two years, I temporarily took over a human resources manager role for a portion of the U.S. work force. I was rewarded for my hard work with a promotion to the human resources manager overseeing the entire division's manufacturing and distribution. I kept working hard and the promotions kept coming.

Over the next decade, I worked top human resources jobs in the United States, Europe and Japan. I had responsibility for human resources in countries around the world, from Poland to South Africa to Israel. Finally, I moved back to the States to assimilate a recently purchased company in Arizona. I was vice president of human resources at a Fortune 300 company. My grandfather was right, bless him.

But a little over a year into my new role in Arizona, something again did not feel quite right. Something was missing, but what? After eleven years and a blizzard of promotions, I realized I missed my planned exit ramp. Not that I ever wanted to get off the amazing and exciting highway I was on at the time, but my hard work and success distracted me from thinking about and doing other things in my life that I really loved. I hadn't considered the possibility of finding a situation in life where I could do it all.

While long hours may be required, <u>successful people spend their time on the right things</u> and in the right roles. When all these factors align, most can't explain how hard or how long they worked. For them it is not a question of how many hours they put in during a week or their work/life balance, but about doing what they love as much as possible.

PAUSE NOW and reflect:

How can I combine all I love to do and make the money I need and want doing it?

Please rate the statement below:

I don't consider how I make my living "work".

Strongly Disagree 1 2 3 4 5 *Strongly Agree*

Remember to sleep on it.

SETTING
YOUR
COURSE

Chapter 20

EXPERIMENT!

> Everything you've ever wanted
> is on the other side of fear.
> – George Addair

Life is full of options so experiment with them. When I was little my parents encouraged me to try every flavor of ice cream before declaring my favorites. And I did, finally settling on chocolate, rocky road and mint chip.

I've also tried many different activities to find my interests. Along the way, I discovered what I excelled at and what I most loved to do. Early in life, Legos, electronics, architecture and woodworking scored high on my list. Later in life, I added business, leadership, theatre and film.

While I always loved music, I have come to terms with the fact that I don't have any natural talent for it. After six years of struggling through private piano lessons, two years of acoustic guitar and a year of being unsuccessfully tutored by my grandfather on harmonica,

I resigned myself to the fact that I would never become the next Chopin or any other noted musician. Instead, I experimented.

I've worked as a bellhop, a teamster, a Broadway theatre manager and in multiple corporate positions. I've sold everything from men's fragrances to ear-piercing products to VCRs (remember those?). My journey took me from jobs in suburban mini-malls in Southern California to packed, New York City diners to boardrooms across Europe, Asia and Africa. I've lived in over thirty different homes, in four different states and in three different countries.

Many people say I did my fair share of experimenting with career and job options, but I have been trumped by at least two purpose seekers.

In 2008 a Canadian university graduate, Sean Aiken, created *The One-Week Job Project* in an effort to answer the question: "What should I do with my life?" Determined to discover his passion and purpose, he embarked on an experimental journey throughout North America working fifty-two jobs in fifty-two weeks. In 2013, a 29-year-old Brit named Matt Frost did the same in the UK. While this is an extreme and impractical technique for most of us, I respect Aiken's and Frost's courage and determination to try new things while searching for purpose and happiness.

PAUSE NOW and reflect:

List all the jobs you worked in your life. Place an asterisk by the jobs you enjoyed most. Of the ones you asterisked, force-rank the jobs from most-liked to least-liked.

Next make a list of the jobs you always wanted to try, but haven't had the courage or opportunity to attempt. Next to each of these jobs explain why you have not tried them then what is stopping you from attempting them now.

Now force-rank the list of jobs you wanted to try from most interesting to least interesting.

Develop an action plan and timeline to try your top job of interest – even if it is for only a few hours after your current day job or on a weekend. Work your way down your list until you have had a chance to try each job.

Take note of why you liked or disliked each new job and also if you wanted to try any of the jobs again.

Please rate the statement below:

I am in a job and career that I love.

Strongly Disagree 1 2 3 4 5 *Strongly Agree*

Remember to sleep on it.

Chapter 21

FINDING YOUR WHY

> Your perception is your reality.

Nancy was friendly, talkative, knowledgeable, hard-working, and engaging — a delightful person. She personally met every job candidate and customer that visited her office. She considered herself the face of her company. When I asked her what she was paid to do, she responded, "to ensure that everyone I speak to and meet with wants to work for or do business with my company." Nancy was a receptionist.

In 1962 while US President Kennedy was touring NASA space center he asked a janitor sweeping the floor what he did for the organization. The man replied, "I'm helping put a man on the moon, Mr. President." And he did.

At the maternity ward of Scottsdale Healthcare in Arizona employees take delight in bringing babies into the world. The sound of a lullaby fills the hallways every time a child is born. Employees stop and smile when this happens. Everyone in every job at the facility feels they contribute to bringing new life into the world. How marvelous is that?

In the day-to-day grind of any job, you can lose focus on why you were hired. <u>By changing your perspective, you can change your life.</u>

Instead of looking at your role as just a job to pay the bills, start looking at the WHY behind your job. WHY does your organization exist in the first place? How does your job support your organization's reason for being? How does your purpose support your job's purpose? Once you determine these things, change your perspective to focus exclusively on your WHY (your purpose). WHY am I here doing what I am doing? It will change your job, career and life.

What's <u>your</u> WHY? If you are having difficulty answering this question, check out Y Scouts' website at yscouts.com for some great examples. Y Scouts is a purpose-based executive search firm leading the way in aligning job seekers with their purpose.

PAUSE NOW and reflect:

WHY does my organization exist?

How does my job support my organization's WHY?

How does my WHY support my job's WHY?

Remember to sleep on it.

Chapter 22

STAYING ON PURPOSE

> Your time is limited, so don't waste
> it living someone else's life.
> – Steve Jobs

While gaining confidence and courage to choose a new path or job is always easier said than done, when it comes to true engagement, staying on purpose is your only choice – the alternative is unacceptable.

Martin Scorsese's 2011 film *Hugo*, which tells the story of a boy who lives alone in a Paris railway station searching for a message from his deceased father, captures this need beautifully. In a moving monologue to a female companion, Hugo opines, "Everything has a purpose, even machines. Clocks tell the time. Trains take you places. They do what they're meant to do. Maybe that's why broken machines make me so sad. They can't do what they're meant to do. Maybe it is the same with people. If you lose your purpose, it's like you're broken."

Kevin Hall's insightful book *Aspire: Discovering Your Purpose Through the Power of Words* concludes that those who follow their true path and purpose have five things in common:

1) They are able to read the clues that guide them on their path

2) They are very clear about where they are going

3) They recognize and embrace their natural gifts

4) They are willing to sacrifice to make significant contributions

5) They follow their bliss

Let's briefly walk through the above points to help you better understand the tools available for embracing your life of purpose.

1)   If you were not born with the natural perception to see and recognize the clues on your path, you will need to intentionally look for these clues each day. Ask others to help you see what you may be missing. In many cases, such clues are apparent by simply being aware of the need to look for them. In my chapter, Keeping Your Eyes and Ears Open, I will share additional tools with you to help in this area.

2) Clarity about your path and needs in the future will be gained from completing the exercises in this book and following through on the goals you set.

3) The Clifton Strengths Finder® tool I described will help you understand and embrace what you do best. Please see Additional Resources in the TOOLS TO HELP YOU section of this book for more information on this valuable tool.

4) Committing to making sacrifices in life for the greater good is fully within your control. It all starts with recognizing your service to others is equal to your returns in life. The more you give, the more you will get. This is a natural law of the universe and it works. Try it for the next 30 days and you will experience first-hand its transforming properties.

5) This book is designed to help you discover and follow your bliss. Two key questions highlighted in this book will help serve as a first step: *If I didn't need money, what would I do in life?* and *What gets me out of bed in the morning?*

My S.L.A.M. model will also help keep you on your path of purpose.

PAUSE NOW and reflect:

Are there important clues I am ignoring in life? If so, why and what are they?

Please rate the statement below:

I know where I am going and where I want to end up in life.

Strongly Disagree 1 2 3 4 5 *Strongly Agree*

Remember to sleep on it.

Chapter 23

UNEXPECTED HELP
FROM OTHERS

> Ask and it will be given to you;
> seek and you will find; knock and
> the door will be opened to you.
> – Jesus, Matthew 7:7

When you know where you need to go in life and open the door to start your journey, people will be waiting on the other side to help you.

When I opened my door to purpose, the first person waiting for me was Brendon Burchard, a personal development trainer, helping those interested in teaching others. I wanted to continue my mission of helping others to be successful and happier by teaching them how to find a job, career and life they love. Just as I was doing.

After completing his six-week online course, I boarded a plane to attend his live event in Santa Clara, CA just outside of San Francisco. There I deepened my knowledge on how to effectively teach others what I knew about jobs and careers.

Brendon's course turned out to be a wonderful, life-changing experience in more ways than one. While Brendon's top line mission was to tactically help me learn the most effective ways to make a living as a writer and teacher, his secondary - and more important mission - was to help me better understand the purpose behind my own mission to teach others. Through the course I also came to understand my story.

The event proved to be a very emotional journey right when I needed it most. I laughed, danced, hugged, cried and met some remarkable people in a group of about eight hundred attendees from all over the world. The room overflowed with love, passion, support and inspiration. Most of the attendees were already wildly successful in life and were now looking to take things to a new level or perhaps in a completely different direction. I met doctors, psychologists, CEO's, best-selling authors, successful entrepreneurs, life coaches, artists, filmmakers, actors, an energy healer and a psychic - you name it!

But my "a-ha moment" came from an unexpected person at a very unforeseen time on the evening of the second day. The long, emotional day wore me out. I wanted to grab a quick dinner and then retire to my room for a bit of writing and a quick FaceTime call with my wife and two little daughters.

In an effort to avoid the seminar attendees at the hotel, I snuck out the hotel's side door, seeking out the Japanese restaurant across the street. Much to my dismay, I was immediately recognized by several of the event attendees sitting at a table together. They offered to add a chair for me. I quickly responded by telling them not to worry as the table was already quite packed with little room for another person. It was not that I did not enjoy the company of the people I was meeting at the event – I truly did and found them all incredibly inspirational – I just needed some down time to clear my head and think about life.

Just as I was about to maneuver myself to an out-of-the-way table for two, a lone voice from a booth next to the group said, "You can join me." Desperate to get out of socializing when I was very tired and hungry, I responded by asking if he was a seminar attendee and hoping he would say no so I could sit by myself. I was not so lucky. "Yes." He gestured to the empty bench across from him. I resigned myself to the fact that I wouldn't get my quick meal that evening unless I wanted to appear extremely rude, something I simply didn't have in me.

Robert was half way through his meal, but was very interested in getting to know me. In my state of sleep and food deprivation, and self-reflection, I experienced difficulty being articulate. Words came out of my mouth, but my mind drifted elsewhere. I shared my interest in helping others, my love of writing, my passion for the arts and my background in it. I covered my successes in corporate America, my global travels and I raved about my family. I told him about my desire to tie all my passions, talents, strengths and experience into a single focus that would provide me with a further level of fulfillment in life.

I explained I wanted to transition from good to great. I also shared some of my perceived barriers: money, family, lifestyle and what others thought of my plans. I covered my false starts and part-time efforts to follow my chosen path. Everything I shared were things I hoped to work on during Brendon's four-day life improvement workshop.

Robert listened closely and asked me questions along the way about things I had done. Robert had enjoyed massive success as an entrepreneur and investor. He was also a disciple of Tony Robbins and part of his Platinum Partnership program, an honor bestowed on only one hundred people in the world who can afford personal time with the renowned self-help guru.

During our dinner, Robert told me about his failed marriages and his success with his fourth wife, his business ventures and his teachings from Tony.

I've always built my relationships on personal, open book sharing because I experienced first-hand how such a practice builds strong relationships quicker and fosters a sense of trust. By Robert's level of openness, it was obvious he subscribed to the same belief. We learned a lot about each other's lives rather quickly.

Robert shared how Tony would frequently say unexpected and out of context things to throw his disciples off their game. By doing this, Robert explained, Tony disoriented his clients, leaving them vulnerable to suggestions about how they view their life and world.

I listened intently despite my state of mind. The topic interested me and fed my core desire to help others find happiness in life.

After dinner, we paid the bill and walked the ten minutes back to the hotel together. During the walk, Robert started pushing me a bit into an uncomfortable conversation. When I said I was really enjoying the event, but probably would not spend the money on another one, he asked me why not, if it added value to my life.

I didn't have a good answer.

He asked me if I had done anything with the online course materials I had already been through.

"Not yet," I said.

"Why not?"

"Well, I have a lot of things going on right now." I started to go down my list. Robert jumped back in.

"Why don't you try to implement what you learned to determine if it adds value to you before making a decision not to spend any more money on such programs?"

Again, a good point, but he was starting to become a bit of a jerk. I barely knew the guy and he was attacking everything I said.

Reaching the hotel lobby, I felt relieved knowing in seconds the elevator would deposit me near my room where I could finally be alone.

But Robert was not quite done with me.

"You are in the middle of the road," he said, "you just need to get the fuck to the other side."

"What?! Who the hell are you?!" was what I *thought*, but what I *said* was, "Good point. I hear what you are saying."

Again, Robert fired back.

"You are in your head. It is obvious. You are using phrases like 'I am trying,' 'I am working on it,' 'Good point,' 'I hear what you are saying.' You are making excuses. Just do it. Even your body language is telling me you are pent up inside."

Now things seemed to be getting way too personal. I started defending myself saying I had already made many bold moves in my life to get to where I was today.

Thinking that was all, I moved to shake Robert's hand. He hadn't finished turning my world upside down.

"What does a bold move deserve? Another bold move? What do you expect to happen next?" then Robert shot his final bullet, "This is why you have not been successful. You have limited your potential. Imagine what you could do, if you focused on the right things in life."

Then he gave me a hug and left.

As I rode the elevator up to my room, wondering what had just happened, I thought to myself, "How could he have said that? He barely knows me. I have been wildly successful in my career.

I worked on Broadway, was a VP at a Fortune 300 company, the head of a global charity, lived all over the world, made great money and wrote for *Forbes*. Limiting my success? This guy is crazy."

But the whole conversation rattled my cage more than I knew. When I called my wife, I broke down as I told her what happened. She asked me why I was so upset.

"He is right," I said.

What Robert heard me say was I knew I could do more with my life, but I was afraid to take action. He heard me talk about my talents, strengths, passions, desires and then make excuses why I wouldn't take a chance, pulling everything together to experience <u>real</u> success.

What Robert was really saying to me was, "Look at what you have been doing – bits of things you are good at and things you like – but imagine what you could do, if you <u>focused entirely on what you are great at and what you love</u>."

Robert told me I needed to change my strategy in life or I would continue to fall short of my true potential and happiness.

His words were hard to hear, but this man changed the way I looked at my career, job and life. And he knew it.

Once my full efforts were focused on what I do best and love, things started to happen for me. A week later I was offered a paid contract from *Forbes* to produce more articles for them (my first contract was unpaid). Two weeks after that, I received an email from *Huffington Post* asking me if I would be interested in writing for them. After a few days more, a friend's referral led to an offer from HR.com to publish my work and present to their membership of over 220,000 people. Next, I fielded call after call and email after email from people wanting to help me or to refer me to someone who could. I was also asked for an interview on HuffPost Live.

It was remarkable – a dream come true.

I discovered something that has been true since Jesus' time and before: knock on your door of purpose and people will be waiting on the other side to answer and to help you.

You are not alone on your path to find your purpose. Those around you can provide guidance, support, or simply a smile to encourage you as you strive for change. Your family and friends are an important resource during your transition to a new job or career and life. I will cover more on that subject in the chapter Balancing Family.

In my *Forbes* article *One Interview Question You Should Ask Every Candidate*, I discussed missing lunch, something that frequently happens when I'm writing. Sometimes I write through the night despite the fact I was tired at 11PM. I lose track of time because the writing I do hits all my positive buttons: strength, talent, passion and purpose. Writing is something I love and needs to be a part of my life – it captures all of me.

What captures all of you?

PAUSE NOW and reflect:

When in my life have I been so passionately focused on an activity that I lost track of time and what was I doing?

Please rate the statement below:

I am interested in and speak enthusiastically about what I am currently doing in life.

Strongly Disagree 1 2 3 4 5 *Strongly Agree*

Remember to sleep on it.

Chapter 24

YOU CAN BECAUSE . . .

> I attribute my success to this:
> I never gave or took any excuse.
> – Florence Nightingale

My grandfather on my mother's side was an extremely successful, hard-driving and courageous man. During the Depression, he lived with his wife in their car for a time, but he never stopped dreaming of a better life. With his last two thousand dollars he turned his trade into his own plumbing and heating business and eventually built it into a multi-million dollar company. He expanded his holdings by purchasing two shopping centers. During his life, he donated large sums to charities.

While some businessmen jumped off bridges in despair and others resigned themselves to poverty, my grandfather spent the Great Depression looking for ways he could make a difference.

As a child, if I ever said, "I can't because . . ." he would say, "You can because . . ."

He never made excuses.

Another example close to my heart, comes from a dear friend of mine who happened to be my theatrical directing mentor at California State University, Fullerton. He recently shared how blessed he felt to have spent his whole life and career doing what he loves: directing theatre and teaching others how to do it. At the age of eighty, after a recent heart attack, he is still one of the most active and happy people I know. An email he sent me today explains why:

". . . have been running around all day and just got in -- and have to go out again tonight. Am looking to buy a three-wheeled bicycle -- the kind with basket in the back and need to get it soon. I cannot ride a 2 wheeler because I don't dare fall -- that would be catastrophic. We have a new puppy and he needs exercise. So with a 3 wheeler I can ride and he can run."

My friend, Dean, never sees barriers in life, just solvable challenges. The way he sees life is why he has always been able to do what he loves – he makes no excuses as to why it can't be done. Today, the accessibility of technology can eliminate any excuse as to why something can't be done. Computer users can quickly and affordably set up websites, then market their offerings for free on social media platforms like Facebook, Twitter, Google and LinkedIn. They can also collect payment from customers on easy to use, secure networks and get assistance from designers, programmers, developers, writers, marketers and others around the world from websites like Elance.com.

If you are searching for outside funding, seek no strings attached funding from investors on sites like Kickstarter.com for anything from film projects to technology endeavors.

A quick search of the web will highlight people making a great living (full-time and part-time) doing what they love – writing, knitting, gardening, cooking, baking, designing, teaching, training or whatever else you can imagine. These people are stay-at-home moms and dads, students, retired professionals, entrepreneurs and ex-executives, all pursuing their dreams and purpose and eating well doing it.

More organizations are getting on board with the idea of employees pursuing their dreams and purpose. They further engage their workforce through corporate work flexibility, making side pursuits easier to run while still maintaining a full time job at the same level of engagement. But remember, being aligned with your organization's purpose as well will offer you the best of both worlds.

PAUSE NOW and reflect:

What excuses am I making about not being able to have a job, career and life I love?

Please rate the statement below:

I don't make excuses in life.

Strongly Disagree 1 2 3 4 5 *Strongly Agree*

Remember to sleep on it.

Chapter 25

STRATEGY IS EVERYTHING

> If the wind will not serve,
> take to the oars.
> – Latin Proverb

My business at LouisEfron.com is a result of changing strategy. I have been writing ever since I was able to put pencil to paper. I always dreamed of being published and writing a book. When my articles were published on Forbes.com it was a dream come true. (Actually, being published anywhere was a dream come true. *Forbes* just made it extra special.)

When my first article appeared on Forbes.com, I had about three hundred views in the first two hours. I was beside myself. Up until that moment, no more than fifty people had seen my writing in my whole life. Over the moon, I sent an email to one of the editors at *Forbes* asking if this was common for a new writer to get so many readers so quickly. I think she thought I was mad. Three hundred readers was hardly anything to celebrate for an article on *Forbes*. From my perspective, I had arrived.

Since then, my articles have been viewed and read by millions of people around the world, but I also realized my strategy was too focused on getting published. I wasn't thinking about how I was going to earn a living as a writer. I was writing articles for *Forbes* and then *Huffington Post* for free while working feverishly on my book. But the whole time I lost sleep over how to pay my bills.

I decided to look online for help. That's when I discovered Brendon Burchard and his course, Total Product Blueprint, on how to make a living teaching others what I knew. After watching a few of his introductory videos, I realized that this was the strategy piece I was missing. I needed to start thinking about my writing and book - not only as things personally fulfilling and helpful to others - but as a business to support my family long-term.

This change in strategy expanded my thinking into other products I could offer (workbooks, audio programs, video training, speaking events, etc.) to help more people than I imagined previously. Ultimately, these products would fuel a business, allowing me to do even more of what I wanted to do full time. My change in strategic perspective turned everything around for me. My confidence in the path I had chosen strengthened, further invigorating me.

While I am not advocating that everyone needs to start a business, I am encouraging you to think differently about what you are trying to do, so you can do more of it. I encourage you to reach out to as many people as possible who are successfully doing what you want and need to do. From experience, I know you will be surprised how many people will be willing and happy to help guide you. And the new perspectives you gain will help you hone your strategy, allowing you to do more of what you desire and to fulfill your life purpose.

PAUSE NOW and reflect:

Who else is successfully doing what I want to be doing and what is their strategy?

Please rate the statement below:

I have a successful job, career and life strategy.

Strongly Disagree 1 2 3 4 5 *Strongly Agree*

Remember to sleep on it.

TAKING THE
FIRST STEP

Chapter 26

GETTING IT RIGHT

> Definiteness of purpose is the starting
> point of all achievement.
> – W. Clement Stone

In the year 2000, the online dating site eHarmony launched with the tag line "Beat the odds, Bet on Love with eHarmony." It pioneered a new scientific approach to matching couples, relying on pre-assessments to gain a deep understanding of its clients and compatibilities before any pictures or profiles were shared by individuals. This concept changed relationship-matching forever and improved chances of successful dating, marriage and fulfilling, long-term partnerships.

In such a process there is no gaming the system, no imagined personas, because neither side knows of the other's existence until a personal match is made. This same concept will ultimately revolutionize job search and placement for the next workforce generation looking for purpose over work.

Arizona based Y Scouts - a company I mentioned earlier and that I recently started partnering with to place my purpose-based job seekers - operates an executive search model similar to eHarmony's dating process. However, the dating site is contemplating offering a non-executive job search option soon. Until then, non-executives must be definitive in purpose, proactive, plus ask targeted questions (like the ones in this book) and effectively process answers. Paying special attention to clues will also help guide your future path.

PAUSE NOW and reflect:

You should have the answers to the questions below prior to starting your job search. Stay true to them while applying to positions. If you are working with a recruitment agency, share the questions, and your answers, with them before they introduce roles to you. Ask them to connect you only to organizations and jobs that are a clear fit.

NOTE: You may have already thought about and answered some of the questions below earlier in this book. If so, you can simply use those answers for this section.

What job would I be excited to share with others?

What kind of organizational purpose would inspire me to share it with others?

What gets me out of bed in the morning?

If I didn't need money, what would I do in life?

What do I do best?

What am I most passionate about?

What am I most interested in?

What have I most enjoyed doing throughout my life and why?

Please rate the statement below:

I am always true to myself.

Strongly Disagree 1 2 3 4 5 *Strongly Agree*

Remember to sleep on it.

Chapter 27

FOCUS

> Where focus goes energy flows.
> – Tony Robbins

This book and my purpose-based business is a direct result of focus. By using the process described in this book myself, I determined the path I wanted and needed to be on. Then I committed everything I had to make it work – including selling my family home to finance my journey.

Despite my full commitment and innate optimism, I battled self-doubt, along with some unhelpful remarks from others. The types of comments I could have done without included "You make good money, have a nice home, cars, a family to take care of – don't screw it up." The high-paying corporate job opportunities sent my way were appreciated, but they also forced me to take another deep breath before letting them pass into my rearview mirror. A U-turn would have been counterproductive; I had come so far. People inquiring about my "back-up plan" made me a bit paranoid. Despite this, and some frustrating conversations, I refused to adopt such negative thinking. I had seen the results of people who expected to fail. They always did.

I am not saying you should pursue a job, career and life change without having a safety net in place. I was lucky enough to have several life preservers: enough equity in my home, a retirement fund for a loan if things became dire, the opportunity to take another decent paying job and the support of my loving wife who was willing to endure a major lifestyle adjustment while I made my transition. While I realize not everyone is as lucky, I was strategic about my moves both when I had money and when I didn't. I looked to maximize my positives and limit my risks, but always pushed myself outside my comfort zone. If you look deep enough, there are always options to make something work. If you focus on failing, you will.

I knew I was on the right path and needed to stay focused on my course and purpose in life. Instead of backing down by taking the easy and comfortable route of simply going back to any high-paying corporate job to pay the bills, I kept my focus and readjusted my strategy, as needed. I evolved into a new and better me.

II

PAUSE NOW and reflect:

What am I most focused on and is my focus in the right place?

Please rate the statement below:

My life focus is making me happy and successful.

Strongly Disagree 1 2 3 4 5 *Strongly Agree*

Remember to sleep on it.

Chapter 28

CONFIDENCE TO LIVE A HAPPY AND FULFILLED LIFE

> Believe you can and you're halfway there.
> – Theodore Roosevelt

Humans are born with complete confidence. My best proof: my 10-month-old daughter. Her walk is shaky, she constantly falls down and she can't really communicate – aside from being really upset at feeding time. Still, she never thinks twice about getting up after a fall to navigate across a room to interact with others.

She is not special in these behaviors. Most healthy babies raised in a happy, comfortable environment can retain their confidence well into their childhood. As babies, they have not learned to lack confidence in their abilities, be nervous when addressing others, or be anxious when all the attention is focused on them.

Unfortunately, confidence can be stripped away by our experiences and outside influences as we age. We remember past failures. We second-guess ourselves. We hunch our shoulders in embarrassment or defeat. Our learned lack of self-confidence is harmful to pursuing the job, career and life we desire.

To make matters worse, research shows on average, interviewers reach final decisions about applicants only four minutes after meeting them. That is barely enough time to evaluate how you look and speak, how you carry yourself and how you greeted the interviewer – all clues of your level of self-confidence.

I'm not suggesting that your skills, experience and personal relationships amount to nothing, but being confident will maximize these qualities. Being comfortable with your abilities and position in all aspects of your life will not only increase your odds of landing a great job, it will make you happier and healthier.

The good news is confidence can be generated and regained. Here's how:

Power Posing

In Amy Cuddy's video, *Your Body Language Shapes Who You Are*, she asserts not only does body language affect how others see you, but also how we see ourselves. Her studies show that "Power Posing" – standing in a posture of confidence, even when you don't feel confident – affects your brain's testosterone and cortisol levels. This stance makes you feel more confident. Her research concludes that changing your body positions also influenced how others see you. Power Posing immediately before an interview or important meeting – or before any event where you are in need of a confidence boost – will greatly improve how you feel and appear to others. Power Posing can be done anywhere you feel comfortable doing it – a restroom, stairwell, or an empty elevator. I frequently do it backstage before a presentation or before the cameras role when filming.

The Confidence Mirror

In a Radford University publication, *Behavioral Interviews: It's Not What You Know it's What You Did*, confidence is strongly correlated to attractiveness. Multiple studies also concluded that "attractive" people get more offers and make more money. Making yourself attractive during an interview or other interaction with a comfortably firm handshake, direct eye contact, good posture, relaxed but passionate communication style, plus a genuine smile will give you an edge.

Body Positioning

You can naturally adjust your body for confidence by asking yourself, "If I was really interested in what I was hearing and seeing, how would I sit?" You will be surprised how often you must readjust your body at important times in life and how much more confident you feel afterwards.

Affective Memory

As a theatre director, I used a technique called Affective Memory to help my actors connect with their characters and generate a consistent, real and confident performance. This process is a central part of Method Acting, a system pioneered by the late Russian theatre director and actor, Constantin Stanislavski, which requires actors to call on personal memory details from a similar situation to those of their characters. Used with positive personal experiences, this same technique can be effectively applied to rehearsals for job interviews and other important meetings on your path to the job, career and life you love.

PAUSE NOW and reflect:

Schedule ten minutes in your day. Find a quiet and comfortable place where you won't be interrupted, mute your phone and other distracting devices and try the below exercise. Experience the interaction in your head, heart and hands – live it and rehearse it, as needed.

Recall an experience when you gave a firm and confident handshake. Close your eyes. See the eyes and face of a friendly and kind person you know or previously met. Hear their reassuring words. Feel the energy of a positive and successful interaction, meeting, interview or past exchange. Pay attention to what your posture, breathing and heartbeat were like at that time. Mimic them now.

Done completely, this exercise provides confidence for your upcoming interview and interaction by connecting the current event to positive and successful experiences you experienced already in your life. You will no longer be walking into an unknown and perhaps scary circumstance, but one where you were successful. If done correctly, your mind will not be able to distinguish the difference between the two.

This technique can be effectively applied to all exchanges in your life – even dating.

Mastery

If you are early in your career – or short on experience, knowledge and success – seek development assistance from relevant books, the web, training courses or a mentor. Good resources and a commitment to study will give you the confidence you require.

Exercise and Dress

Staying fit and dressing in a way that makes you feel comfortable and good about yourself are always confidence builders. Both will give you more self-assurance. Regular exercise also provides you more energy and makes you stronger to meet life's challenges.

Clothes don't make you, but they can influence an interviewer's initial impression of you. I'm not advocating buying expensive suits, shoes or purses. But, you need to be aware of your physical appearance. You can easily gain a boost of confidence by wearing your favorite clothing item. You want to be honest and appear as yourself, of course, but you must dress neatly and professionally, in line with the organization and job for which you are interviewing.

Remember to organize your resume or other papers inside something to control clutter. Being and appearing both prepared and organized can help highlight your value as a potential employee. A female friend carries smaller purses to interviews and meetings then tucks them into a business attaché to leave a free hand for that all-important first, confident handshake. It is also important to silence any handheld devices. Even if your phone is on silent, it will distract from your presentation when it lights up or vibrates during your interview so keep it out of sight.

Smile

If interviews, meetings and speeches make you nervous, don't worry; you aren't alone. Take a deep breath and smile. Research shows that smiling can encourage collaboration and productivity in a work environment. Not only that, but smiling helps trick your brain into believing everything is alright even when it's not.

Goal Setting

Achieving goals, even if it is just checking off items on a list, can increase your confidence levels with the satisfaction that you have achieved something worthwhile. Your Purpose M.A.P.™ discussed later in this book will assist you with this, too.

Focus on the Positives

We tend to focus our energies on negative events. Despite buckets of positive experiences, it takes only one or two nasty comments to knock someone off their horse. In fact, meanness is at the root of all confidence issues. Being laughed at when you make a mistake, being harshly rejected by someone you like, or being taunted on a schoolyard, all of these play a part in crushing a person's self-confidence.

To overcome negative experiences in life, focus on positive ones. Most people can count only a handful of truly devastating life experiences, while positive occurrences are abundant.

The late Dr. Maya Angelou once said, "At the end of the day people won't remember what you said or did, they will remember how you made them feel."

We have the ability to give the gift of confidence to everyone we meet by being constructive and kind in all our interactions. I encourage you to be a champion of confidence for others. It not only feels good and helps others, but gives you greater confidence in return.

‖

 PAUSE NOW and reflect:

Make two columns on a page. List all the positive and negative human interactions you can remember from the last twelve months. They can be events as small as a stranger smiling at you or not returning your smile in the street.

Which list is larger? If you are like most, the positive list far outweighs the negative one, highlighting the irrationality of not doing something for fear of one or two negative reactions afterwards. If your negative interactions list outweighs your positive list, you may want to start asking others around you why. Listen closely to their responses and start looking in your own heart for answers.

Rewriting Your Self-Talk

Self-talk is the positive or negative comments that float through our head, or sometimes out of your mouth, as a running monologue throughout your day. They influence how you feel and behave and are usually triggered by events in our lives. If positive, they have magical properties to transform your life and allow you to achieve remarkable things. If negative, they will fulfill their destiny and deliver on your expectations. For example, if you say, "I am fat" or "I look fat", you will feel fat even though you may not appear that way to others. If you say, "I am ugly", you will feel ugly, even though others will not have the same opinion of you. If you say, "I am not good enough", you will never feel good enough. If you say, "I can't speak in front of others", you will never feel confident when public speaking.

Self-talk can be your best friend or your worst enemy. The good news is you get to choose which one. Think positive thoughts and you will get positive outcomes. Think negative thoughts and you will get negative outcomes. It is as simple as that.

The other day, I went running while my five-year-old daughter rode her bike next to me. Halfway through the run we came across a moderately sized hill. My daughter stopped her bike and said, "Daddy, I can't make it up this hill." "Of course you can honey," I assured her. "You just have to believe you can." I told her to say, "I can do it" as she rode her bike successfully up the hill.

A week later at a park I was throwing a football to her. Seeing some tall trees she asked, "Daddy, can you throw the football over that tree?" It was a rather large tree. "Honey, I don't think so. It's quite a tall tree." "Of course you can, Daddy, you just have to believe you can. Just say 'I can do it' as you throw the ball." Well, she was right.

Simply believing that something can be done, can make it so. In the powerful and eternal words of Earl Nightingale, "Believe and succeed."

PAUSE NOW and reflect:

What are your negative self-talk triggers in life (e.g., entering a building for an interview, shaking hands with a stranger, speaking to the opposite sex, interacting with someone you like, respect and admire, or answering questions on topics you are not an expert on)?

Write down your negative self-talk triggers now.

Next, write down what you say to yourself when these events occur and how it makes you feel.

Now, cross out any negative "self-talk" and re-write the statements in a positive and assertive manner – in a way that makes you feel confident and good about yourself when you read and say the statements aloud. In this way you can turn: "This person will never be interested in me" into the positive statement "I am worthy of this person's attention."

By re-writing your self-talk, you will change the way you feel and how you behave. Negative self-talk will generate low self-confidence and self-esteem issues while positive self-talk produces the opposite effect.

Practice positive self-talk throughout your life and your confidence levels will soar.

<u>Be Prepared, Present and Helpful</u>

Other keys to confidence are being prepared when you can, staying present, and being helpful to others. Being prepared gives you confidence so you won't be caught off guard. Even if you are, you will be better prepared to deal with that, too.

Stay connected and fully engaged in whatever you are doing in life, especially when interacting with others. People will feel respected, valued, and important when you are present with them. They will hopefully make you feel the same in return.

Connect with people around you by being helpful to them and genuinely interested in what they have to say. The more focused you are on others, the less room insecurities, nervousness and doubt will have to creep in.

Also, as Jim Rohn - motivational speaker and author of *7 Strategies for Wealth & Happiness* - suggested, "You are the average of the five people you spend the most time with." Spend your time with people who are also present and helpful.

PAUSE NOW and reflect:

How can I be more present in my life?

Remind yourself to be present, when needed. When I find myself drifting from an activity or a conversation I use the power of internal self-talk to bring me back to a present state. "I am focused" does it for me. Experiment to find the word or statement that will work for you.

Please rate the statement below:

I am always present in life.

Strongly Disagree 1 2 3 4 5 *Strongly Agree*

Remember to sleep on it.

ENSURING
ALIGNMENT

Chapter 29

KEEPING YOUR EYES AND EARS OPEN

> Don't look at the ants when there are
> elephants walking by.
> – Anonymous

Recently at a department store, I heard an employee telling a coworker about an upcoming job interview. "They want me to shave my beard, but I don't want to."

"Hmm," I thought, "maybe he should just cancel that interview."

Sure, refusing to shave a beard seems like a trivial – or even childish – reason to lose out on a job. But the employee's emotional attachment to his facial hair is also a red flag for job misalignment.

Every job interview is a window into the organization's culture. If you are asked to make unwanted changes before you even start working for the organization, is the job really for you? In the short amount of time it takes to interview for a position, I guarantee you will see and hear many clues about your future happiness at the organization. Make sure you pay attention to any obvious, personal disconnects.

Below are twelve seemingly small, but hugely important things to consider when searching for your next job. If after reviewing and thinking about your answers you don't feel you will be happy at a particular organization, you probably won't be and should not pursue employment there.

1. Website
2. Job Description
3. Work Location
4. Working Hours
5. Time Off
6. Dress Code
7. Receptionist Interaction
8. Cleanliness
9. Availability
10. Care
11. Acknowledgement (of you and others)
12. Visual Clues

Sometimes the most important information you need about a potential employer is the information in front of your face. I have provided questions for you to consider internally as well as questions to ask your potential employer during the interview process. Decide what is important to you and keep your eyes and ears open while interviewing. Then only accept the job that meets your basic criteria. Also, <u>remember to only seek answers to questions you care about and re-phrase questions, as needed, to make them comfortable for you to ask.</u> Remember the responses you obtain are more important than the way you phrase the question.

When asking questions involving a personal perspective, it is important to ask them multiple times to different people at the organization in order to gain a full picture of what you need to know.

1. WEBSITE

An organization's website can reveal much about company culture and what is important to the people working there. As a human resources professional and writer, I have had numerous organizations interested in telling me about their progressive workplace environments. When I examined some of their websites, there was not a single mention of their employees or culture. If it is not highlighted on their website, you probably won't find it at the organization either.

As you review each potential employer's website you may check off each item below by using the printouts in the TOOLS TO HELP YOU section of this book.

☐ Visit the 'About Us' section of the company website. Study the company history, read any Executive bios and note if the company highlights aspects about their culture.

☐ Read company press releases or other posted news items. *You can also do a simple Google search to find news articles or postings regarding the company.*

☐ Locate articles describing company culture. *Sometimes these links are found on the career page.*

  o Does the company culture fit my needs?

  o Make a note regarding their type of culture and keep that in mind when you go for an interview.

☐ If the company is publically traded you can verify their viability and recent expansion or financial successes/troubles by examining the posted annual report in the 'Investor Relations' pages. Anyone you know at the company can be a very valuable resource for this information, too, especially if it is a privately held organization.

2. JOB DESCRIPTION

A posted job description on the company website or internet job board can inform potential employees about details not only regarding the job, but the company itself. It can also highlight red flags.

I once saw a job description that was ten pages long. It only stopped short of telling candidates how they needed to breathe. A tad too constricting for what I desired.

These items are internal questions for <u>you</u> to answer:

- ☐ Does the job description include requirements like "must have flexible hours" or be a "self-starter with limited guidance"? If so, do these fit with my life and work style?

- ☐ Do they describe the culture by including phrases like "fun environment", "employee should have a sense of humor" or "casual Fridays"? Or is it all business? Which appeals to me?

- ☐ Do they require certifications or college degrees or do they also allow for equivalent work experience?

- ☐ Are there misspellings or confusing language?

3. WORK LOCATION

If you need to relocate or drive a distance to a new office, make sure you are comfortable living in one of the surrounding communities and with the commute. I have withdrawn my name from good job opportunities because my wife and I did not want to live in the area.

These items are internal questions for <u>you</u> to answer:

☐ Do I like the community/area where the job is located?

☐ What is the cost of living in the area (taxes, house prices/rents)?

☐ How far will I need to commute to work and places I enjoy and how convenient will it be?

☐ What are the schools like?

☐ How far will I be from family and friends?

☐ Will I like the weather where I will need to live?

☐ Does the area support the things I like to do in life? *For example, walk, run, bike, hike, ski, dine out, visit museums, see film and live theatre.*

Questions to ask your potential employer:

☐ Will I be required to work in the office or is there a remote working option? *If you don't like being stuck in an office five days a week, don't take a job at an organization that requires this.*

☐ How flexible and results-oriented is the organization's culture? *You will find the greatest flexibility in Results-Only Work Environments. I have included a website in Additional Resources for more information about these organizations.*

☐ What do employees like most about living in [insert job area]?

☐ Where do most employees live?

4. WORKING HOURS

Like vacation time, if personal time outside of work is important to you, find out the normal working hours – <u>not</u> the published working hours. These are frequently separate things. I have worked for organizations claiming their work hours were 9-to-5, but in reality most people worked from 8-to-8. One way to get the scoop about an organization's *real* working hours is to drive by an hour before and after the organization's official work hours to count the cars in the parking lot. If the location is in a big city without accessible parking lots and working hours are important to you, ask the question directly in an interview.

This item is an internal question for <u>you</u> to answer:

☐ If accessible, how early/late do I see cars in the organization's parking lot? *Remember to take into consideration possible night shifts.*

Question to ask your potential employer:

☐ What hours do employees of [insert organization name] traditionally work?

5. TIME OFF

A few months ago, I talked with a friend of mine who values family time more than anything else. Despite this, he accepted a job at a company offering only two weeks of vacation a year, including sick time. With such a stingy time-off policy, the company obviously does not value the same things as my friend. When I recently asked my friend how things were going, he said he probably wouldn't be there long.

You only have one life to live, one chance to fit in everything you need and want to do. Balancing your time is important, especially when it comes to the job you take.

These items are internal questions for <u>you</u> to answer:

☐ Will the organization value and support what I value most in life?

☐ Will this job/organization allow me the time to focus on what is most important to me in life?

Question to ask your potential employer:

☐ One thing(s) that is very important to me in life is
_____. How does [insert organization name] support such interests?

6. DRESS CODE

Being comfortable at work will improve your confidence, productivity and engagement. If you love wearing jeans or shorts and t-shirts to work, don't take a job that requires suits or business attire. If you like wearing suits, you will not be comfortable coming to work in jeans. The more you can be you, the better you'll perform and the happier you'll feel.

These items are internal questions for <u>you</u> to answer:

☐ What were employees wearing when I visited the organization?

☐ Is this the usual attire or was I visiting on a casual Friday?

☐ Am I comfortable with the organization's work attire?

Question to ask your potential employer:

☐ What is the dress code at [insert organization name]?

7. RECEPTIONIST INTERACTION

A receptionist can tell you a lot about the culture of an organization. Even if they are contractors, the first person you meet at any organization should be important to the organization.

If you find the receptionist unfriendly, unhelpful, or clearly disinterested in your presence or their job, take note. Their disengagement may reflect the entire workforce. Pay special attention to how the receptionist interacts with passing employees.

These items are internal questions for <u>you</u> to answer:

☐ Was the receptionist friendly and inviting?

☐ Did the receptionist interact with others passing their work area?

8. CLEANLINESS

Unorganized and un-kept environments can be a sign of much bigger organizational issues like low employee engagement and even ethics problems such as disrespect for company property, rules, policies and laws.

These items are internal questions for <u>you</u> to answer:

☐ What does the lobby look like? Hallways? Offices? Are things clean and well-kept or dirty and unorganized?

☐ Is this the type of working environment that will make me comfortable?

9. AVAILABILITY

Did your interview get rescheduled numerous times or take weeks to book? It could be that all the interviewers are extremely busy or traveling a lot, a key indication of the organization's culture. If it is difficult to pin down your future manager for an interview you may find the same frustration when you need them as an employee.

These items are internal questions for <u>you</u> to answer:

☐ How long did it take to schedule interviews for me?

☐ Did my interview get rescheduled more than once?

Questions to ask your potential employer:

☐ [To your potential manager] How much access will I have to you for assistance, coaching and mentoring?

☐ [To your potential manager] How much interaction do you like to have with your employees? *This question is helpful to ask if you prefer to work closely with your manager or more independently.*

10. CARE

The interest and respect you experience before and during your interview speaks volumes about how you will be treated as an employee.

Once in the interview, did interviewers seem present with you or distracted by others, incoming emails or phone calls? Interviewers who don't care are likely to be managers who don't put a lot of effort into supporting their employees. Were your interviewers prepared for your interview? Preparation is a sign of care for others.

If you are – or you see others – treated poorly or inconsiderately during your interview stage, you can guarantee that it will be magnified by ten when you start working for the organization.

These items are internal questions for <u>you</u> to answer:

☐ Is the company involved in their surrounding community?

☐ Do they sponsor any charities or non-profit groups?

☐ Did I have to wait in the lobby well past my scheduled interview time? If so, did anyone apologize or explain the reason why?

☐ Did my interviewers ask thoughtful questions and let me speak and fully answer what they asked?

☐ Did my interviewers seem present with me or distracted by others, incoming emails or phone calls?

☐ Were my interviewers prepared for my interview and had they reviewed my resume?

☐ Was there anything I saw while visiting the organization that would indicate a lack of care for employees? *For example, unclean restrooms, dirty hallways, smoking allowed in front of all entry doors, poor lighting or working conditions.*

Questions to ask your potential employer:

☐ What types of employee engagement programs does [insert organization name] have?

☐ How do employees usually characterize (or describe) the culture at [insert organization name]?

11. ACKNOWLEDGEMENT (OF YOU AND OTHERS)

Friendly employees are a sign of an engaged workforce.

These items are internal questions for <u>you</u> to answer:

☐ While I was waiting for my interview, did people at the reception desk or in the lobby or hallways acknowledge or interact with me? Were they positive interactions?

□ Did anyone acknowledge me when I walked through the halls to get to my meetings?

Questions to ask your potential employer:

□ What is the employee culture like at [insert organization name]?

□ How are employees recognized at [insert organization name]?

12. VISUAL CLUES

Last year I had the pleasure of touring a progressive software company based in Arizona named Infusionsoft. On my office tour I passed a key ring that read "EGO", hanging on a hook in the lobby. Statements of the company's values and mission were painted on the walls, a banner above an indoor football field reading "We do what we say we'll do," a free cereal bar, a game room, a large open dream room with comfortable sitting areas plus a reference library with a proclamation that read "We believe in people and their dreams" above the entry.

While you'll likely not find as many obvious cultural clues at most organizations, you should be on the lookout for them during your interview. The more signs you see, the stronger the culture will most likely be. You should make a point of asking how these statements and visuals are embraced and lived in the organization.

If you are interviewing at a retail organization, you can usually find a lot of great cultural information near the store's restrooms or employee break rooms. For example, do you see postings about employee recognition programs, community and charity involvement, or employee engagement initiatives? In non-retail environments, the lobby, kitchen areas and above copiers are good places to look. Chances are you will see and hear everything you need to know about the organization while visiting them for interviews. Keep your eyes and ears open and take note.

These items are internal questions for you to answer:

☐ What did I learn about the mission, purpose and values of the organization?

☐ How much can I tell about the organization's culture, mission, purpose and values from being at their location?

☐ Does the organization appear to live its values? *For example, if caring for employees is an organizational value, does the organization have an employee gym, recreation area, meditation rooms, on-site child care and new mother facilities, subsidized meals, generous time off policy, free cereal bar or a dream room?*

☐ Do employees at all levels call each other by their first names or address each other formally?

☐ Do employees eat lunch together or at their desks alone?

☐ Is the organization's culture a culture I am comfortable with and interested in?

Questions to ask your potential employer:

☐ What are the mission, purpose and values of [insert organization name]? *Check the organization's website before your interview to determine if this question is needed. Or rephrase the question to suit, if questions arise after reviewing their website.*

☐ What is most important to the people who work at [insert organization name]?

☐ [To your potential manager] What is most important to you as a manager (or leader) at [insert organization name]?

Once you have completed your interview, review the answers to all your questions. Now you can answer this one:

☐ Based on all the information I have, am I passionate about working for this organization and will I fit into the culture?

Chapter 30

USING A RECRUITER

> It seems to me shallow and arrogant for any man in these times to claim he is completely self-made, that he owes all his success to his own unaided efforts. Many hands and hearts and minds generally contribute to anyone's notable achievements.
>
> – Walt Disney

I was once called to interview for a company where the recruiter warned me not to be late. "The president has a real pet peeve about tardiness," he told me. While I appreciate the importance of being on time for any meeting, the fact that the recruiter made a special point of highlighting this personality trait prior to my interview made me question this boss' rigidity. Personally, I did not want to work where I would have to fear if I was running five minutes late.

In another circumstance, a recruiter apologized to me for an unorganized process and poor follow-up – not the best first impression for any organization and a clear indication of potential engagement and quality of work issues.

A good recruiter will be an invaluable source of important information for you. Ask them as many questions as you can.

These items are internal questions for <u>you</u> to answer:

☐ Was the recruiter positive about the organization (your potential employer) and how much did they know about it and the job?

☐ [For independent recruiters] Did the recruiter give me any indication that they were having trouble dealing with the organization?

Questions to ask your recruiter:

☐ What is the culture like at [insert organization name]? *It is important to ask this question to everybody you speak to regarding the organization to gain varied perspectives.*

☐ What are the demographics of the workforce? *For example: average age, gender, background. This question will help you determine how well you will fit.*

☐ What is most important to [insert organization name]?

☐ What is my potential manager like?

☐ What type of employees work at [insert organization name]?

☐ Do you have a job description to send me?

☐ How long has the job been open and why is it available?

☐ [For independent recruiters] Have you placed others at [insert organization name]? If so, what were the outcomes?

EMBRACING
YOUR FUTURE

Chapter 31

BALANCING FAMILY

> A man travels the world over in search of
> what he needs and returns home to find it.
> – George Moore

I would be remiss not to address the dynamic that family and loved ones have on your journey to find a job, career and life you love. These people are inarguably among the most important factors and influences on your decisions.

The first step in traveling as a family is to share this book with them, explain what you are doing, why you need to do it and where you want and/or need to go. Reveal there may be some bumps along the way. Then ask for their support and love on your journey, comforting them by letting them know this is not a selfish act, but to benefit them, too. <u>For all to be happy we must each be happy.</u>

My lovely wife and I have been married about six years. We have two beautiful, young daughters. During the time we met, started dating and married, my wife knew me only as a corporate executive with good income, benefits and some sense of security. When I decided to transition from a job and make a shift back to my life as an independent writer and businessperson there were understandable concerns.

My wife never knew me as the free-wheeling, independent theatre producer, director and writer living in a studio apartment in NYC and waiting tables on the side to make a living. Needless to say, she was concerned about our children, home, cars, lifestyle and generally how we would live and pay our bills. While supportive of my move to find a better place in life, her concerns created stress for me and tension in our relationship. For her, I was untested outside of corporate America. It was scary.

Despite my confidence, track record of success and eagerness towards a better life, it was incredibly scary for me, too. I now had a family to support, feed and shelter. When I was single, a failed venture simply meant quickly adjusting things in my life to compensate, including where I lived. Things had changed and it was now painfully obvious.

When a partner and family are involved there are only two options: include them on your journey or leave them behind. If you shudder at the thought of leaving your partner, children and other loved ones behind, as I do, there is only one option. You have to engage these people in your process, thinking and decision-making.

It will also be important to give a copy of your Purpose M.A.P.™ to your partner and get their feedback before finalizing it. The Purpose M.A.P.™ will be discussed in detail in a chapter at the end of this book.

While you aren't obligated to change your Purpose M.A.P.™ after your partner reviews it, the success of your plan depends on them feeling part of the process of creating it. You may be surprised by the valuable input you receive.

The importance of leading and teaching by example with children cannot be understated. There is no better gift you can give your children than allowing them to see you happy, present and fulfilled. Your model will pave the way for their success and failures in life.

Ann Landers said it best, "It is not what you do for your children, but what you have taught them to do for themselves, that will make them successful human beings." No pressure!

Chapter 32

YOURS FOR THE TAKING

> Act as if it were impossible to fail.
> – Dorothea Brande

You are the only thing standing between where you are now and the happiness and success you desire. If you think you can't have what you want and need in life, you won't. If you see life as abundant, you will have everything you ever dreamed of. Success in life is for anyone with the courage to pursue it who believes they will achieve it. It is waiting for you, if you want it badly enough. And ironically, the things you want and need most in life are free: love, health, family, friendship, happiness, joy, dreams, support, and encouragement. Money and material things only add joy to your life once you have the things costing you nothing.

I am reminded of a documentary I recently saw called *Escape from a Nazi Death Camp*. In the film, two Jewish detainees at the Nazi death camp Sobibor met, fell in love, escaped, married and had a beautiful family and life together. In the midst of evil, this couple possessed the courage to love and be loved. Their union kept them alive.

Over a century ago, Russell Conwell the Baptist minister and inspirational speaker, encouraged his followers to find the "acres of diamonds" in their own backyards.

At the heart of his message was a parable Conwell recounted about a wealthy man living on a farm by a river.

"He was contented because he was wealthy, and wealthy because he was contented. One day a priest visited the wealthy man and told him about diamonds.

After hearing about the value of the recently discovered stones, the wealthy man now thought himself poor and discontented without them.

He sold his farm, left his family and travelled far to find true wealth – the diamonds. He did not find them and became sick. In despair, he drowned himself in the sea.

Shortly after, the new owner of the man's farm noticed a sparkling stone in a stream on his property. A closer look revealed that it was a diamond. Further excavation uncovered acres of diamonds."

Conwell went on to point out, "You are, at this moment, standing in the middle of your own acres of diamonds." You don't need to travel outside your own heart and mind to find them. But you must be willing to look for them – the price of the diamonds.

The irony is everything you want in the life is attainable and yours for the taking. Your diamonds exist in your ability – the human ability – to appreciate and be content with the riches you have, see the beauty in everything around you, love fully, dream, and serve others who in return will serve you.

A month ago, I had the pleasure of having lunch with Lisa Nichols, the world-renowned transformational author and speaker. During my time with her she was asked how someone could give more of themselves to others. At this question she picked up her water glass and started pouring the contents into her teacup. When the teacup was full, she instructed, most people start serving others when their cup is here – full to the brim. She then continued to pour her water into the teacup until it ran over into the saucer below. She pointed to the water in the saucer and said, "to serve others fully you must serve them from your abundance."

Chapter 33

DEFINE AND DESIGN YOUR LIFE

> When I was 5 years old, my mother always told me that happiness was the key to life. When I went to school, they asked me what I wanted to be when I grew up. I wrote down 'happy'. They told me I didn't understand the assignment and I told them they didn't understand life.
> – Attributed to John Lennon

Sometimes fantasy and fiction are better than the real thing, but not when it comes to living a life of purpose. If you have honestly, thoughtfully and thoroughly answered/rated all the questions/ statements in this book, then analyzed, compared, refined and slept on your responses, you should have a clearer picture of how to define and design your life for happiness, fulfillment and purpose moving forward.

Don't let others do this for you. You get one chance to live your life. Define it, design it, enjoy and fulfill it.

As promised . . . I hope you now have clearer answers for the Purpose Box below. However, as you will come to realize: <u>purpose is a journey, not a destination.</u> Don't despair, if you are still figuring it out.

Chapter 34

YOUR NEXT 30 DAYS+

> A person will reap only what he sows.
> – The Bible, Galatians 6:7

The next thirty days will be very difficult for you. I won't sugarcoat it. The good news is those thirty days will also be life changing. If you commit to what I am about to share with you, your life will be filled with more abundance then you ever imagined.

In Earl Nightingale's 1956 recording entitled *The Strangest Secret*, he defines success as "the progressive realization of a worthy ideal." To be successful in life you must deliberately move in the direction of something you believe to be worthwhile – whatever that is.

PAUSE NOW and reflect:

What is the worthy ideal I am trying to achieve? *This ideal should complement your purpose.*

Nightingale also referenced the noted Psychiatrist Dr. David Harold Fink. Dr. Fink developed the following "6 Steps to Success." As you will discover – when you complete the exercise – they are timeless and life changing. The six steps to success are:

1. Set yourself a definite goal.

2. Quit running yourself down.

3. Stop thinking of all the reasons why you cannot be successful and instead think of all the reasons why you can.

4. Trace your attitudes back through your childhood and discover where you got the idea that you could not be successful if that is the way you've been thinking.

5. Change the image you have of yourself by writing a description of the person you would like to be.

6. Act the part of the successful person you have decided to become.

YOUR 30 DAY+ CHALLENGE:

With Dr. Fink's "6 Steps to Success" in mind, write a description of the person you would like to be. This exercise is not about creating an ulterior persona or character for you to play, but is about being completely true to yourself – being you in every sense.

For the next thirty days, be the person you have decided to become without exception. Don't waver and don't doubt yourself. Have complete confidence in the person you are now and live every aspect of your life that way for the next thirty days.

If you find yourself slipping back into your old ways, start your thirty days over again. At the end of thirty days, if you love the person you have become and are succeeding in life, repeat this exercise for another thirty days, and so on. There will come a point where you will no longer have to think about this new person or this exercise. You will have become that person and you will be living the life you only dreamed previously.

Start now. Your life awaits you!

Chapter 35

YOUR PURPOSE M.A.P.™

> Whatever the mind of man can conceive and
> believe, it can achieve.
> – Napoleon Hill

Congratulations on coming this far! Now it's time to bring it all together.

In this chapter I will introduce the Purpose Master Action Plan™ (your Purpose M.A.P.™). Your Purpose M.A.P.™ is the tool you will use to action what you have learned and discovered throughout this book. It is a simple tool intended to work in conjunction with your 30 Day+ Challenge creating an actionable roadmap to make your purpose-driven life a reality.

There are ten questions on Your Purpose M.A.P.™ to help you move through a 30-day action plan in parallel with your 30 Day+ Challenge. I will show you sample answers on page 165 for clarification.

The questions are:

1. What is my current Purpose Alignment Indicator Score™*?

2. What is my definitive statement about the difference I am trying to make in the world – my purpose (Chapter 33)?

3. What is the worthy ideal I am trying to achieve (Chapter 34)?

4. What is the description of the person I have decided to become (Chapter 34)?

5. What is my 30-Day goal(s) to support my purpose, worthy ideal and me (Be sure to make this answer S.M.A.R.T. - see page 163)?

6. What is my 30-Day action(s) to achieve my goal(s)?

7. What is my 30-Day outcome(s)?

8. What is my new Purpose Alignment Indicator Score™?

9. Has my Purpose Alignment Indicator Score™ changed for the better or worse?

10. What do I need to action on my next 30-Day Purpose M.A.P.™ to improve my purpose alignment?

After answering all the ten questions and completing your 30-Day Purpose M.A.P.™, I encourage you to create a new Purpose M.A.P.™ for your next thirty days, and so on. If you follow this on-going process, you will create a structured, goal attainment discipline to ignite success in your life.

*In question number one of your Purpose M.A.P.™, you will record your Purpose Alignment Indicator Score™. To determine your score, total all the end-of-chapter statement rating numbers you circled in this book, beginning with Chapter 2, then divide that number by 27 (the number of relevant, rated statements).

As a reminder, your Purpose Alignment Indicator Score™ can also be obtained electronically by completing the Purpose Alignment Indicator Survey™ on my website at LouisEfron.com.

Purpose Alignment Indicator Score™ Scale:

Examine your Purpose Alignment Indicator Score™ results and compare them to the list below. Your results will show where you stand on the path to living your purpose.

4+ = Strong Purpose Alignment
You are happy, fulfilled and purpose-driven
Ongoing self-development and reflection are important

3.5 to 3.99 = Moderate Purpose Alignment
Further analysis, thought and strategy revision may be needed
Purpose coaching helpful

3 to 3.49 = Low Purpose Alignment
Further analysis, thought and strategy development may be needed
Purpose coaching recommended

Less than 3 = Little to No Purpose Alignment
Purpose coaching recommended

If you are interested in purpose coaching based on this book, please email me at Louis@LouisEfron.com.

When completing your Purpose M.A.P.™ be sure to make all your goals S.M.A.R.T.

A S.M.A.R.T. goal is defined as one that is Specific, Measurable, Achievable, Results-focused and Time-bound.

Below is a definition of each of the S.M.A.R.T. goal criteria you will use when completing your Purpose M.A.P.™.

Specific: what you are going to do stated in a simple and clear way.

Measurable: a measure that provides clear evidence of what you accomplished. For example, if your specific goal is to raise more money for a charitable cause, how much had you raised when you drafted your goal and how much more did you raise at your next milestone? Any measure that will allow you to track and define your improvements will work.

Achievable: something you can truly accomplish with a stretch.

Results-focused: the return that will be gained from your efforts.

Time-bound: the timeframe in which your action(s) will be completed.

When I decided to trade my career in the arts for a corporate one, I created a Purpose M.A.P.™ to achieve my goal. By way of example, mine is on the next page.

SAMPLE PURPOSE M.A.P.™	
NAME: Louis Efron	DATE: September 2000
QUESTIONS	ANSWERS
1. What is my current Purpose Alignment Indicator Score™?	*I had not yet developed this tool.*
2. What is my definitive statement about the difference I am trying to make in the world – my purpose (Chapter 33)?	*To enlighten, inspire, and teach . . . to help others see the possibilities in life.*
3. What is the worthy ideal I am trying to achieve (Chapter 34)?	*To improve employee engagement and make people happier in their jobs.*
4. What is the description of the person I have decided to become (Chapter 34)?	*A corporate labor relations specialist and an expert in my field. A person always focused in my efforts to help others grow and succeed.*
5. What is my 30-Day goal(s) to support my purpose, worthy ideal and me (Make this S.M.A.R.T.)?	*To get an employment offer as a corporate labor relations specialist at an organization that helps improve the lives of others within 30 days. To increase my total compensation by 50%.*
6. What is my 30-Day action(s) to achieve my goal(s)?	*Create a corporate labor relations specialist resume. Apply for six labor relation's jobs on Monster.com every day with a focus on the medical industry.*
7. What is my 30-Day outcome(s)?	*I received an offer from a Fortune 500 medical device company as a labor relations specialist. I doubled my total compensation.*
8. What is my new Purpose Alignment Indicator Score™?	*I had not yet developed this tool.*
9. Has my Purpose Alignment Indicator Score™ changed for the better or worse?	*I had not yet developed this tool.*
10. What do I need to action on my next 30-Day Purpose M.A.P.™ to improve my purpose alignment?	*I had not yet developed this tool.*
Create a new 30-Day Purpose M.A.P.™ now	

Go to LouisEfron.com now to download your Purpose M.A.P.™ template for the below exercise. I have included the template in the TOOLS TO HELP YOU section, too.

You may address multiple goals on a 30-Day Purpose M.A.P.™ as long as they are reasonably achievable. Quality is more important than quantity in this exercise. If you repeatedly set goals that you can't and don't achieve, you will quickly become discouraged.

For this exercise, it is helpful to have the answers to all your questions/statements and your responses/ratings (those you answered in the Purpose Boxes in each chapter of this book) in front of you for review. Please locate them now, then answer the below questions as you complete your own Purpose M.A.P.™:

What are the themes I see throughout my responses to the questions/statements in this book? *List them now.*

Thinking about all the questions/statements I answered/rated in this book, what decisions and commitments can I now make about my job, career and life?

▶ After you have thought about, slept on and completed your Purpose M.A.P.™ ask the following questions:

What can I do to make my Purpose M.A.P.™ most successful?
Make the needed revisions on your Purpose M.A.P.™ now.

Is my Purpose M.A.P.™ S.M.A.R.T.?
If you are struggling with your Purpose M.A.P.™, go back to the questions/statements and your answers/ratings, think about and sleep on them further and review, answer and sleep on additional questions as needed in the Supplemental Purpose Questions section at the back of this book. You may create your own questions to further refine your Purpose M.A.P.™ to your needs. If you are not connected personally, emotionally and intellectually to your Purpose M.A.P.™ revisions are needed.

Once you feel confident about your Purpose M.A.P.™ . . .

ACTION IT, KEEP ON TRACK WITH S.L.A.M. AND
NEVER AGAIN LIVE A LIFE OF REGRETS!

Even though I designed this book to help guide your independent thinking, it is highly beneficial to share your question responses, statement ratings and your initial Purpose M.A.P.™ with a group of people you trust and respect. The additional insight and guidance from those who know you best will be extremely valuable to you.

Thank you for your commitment to this book, for being you and for wanting to make a difference in your life and the world. I wish you an abundance of success.

Have fun, be happy and live on purpose!

TOOLS TO
HELP YOU

PURPOSE BOX QUESTIONS

(Also available as a download at LouisEfon.com to be
used as you read this book.)

GETTING STARTED

Chapter 1:   What do I believe to be my purpose in life (i.e., my definitive statement about the difference I am trying to make in the world)?

Chapter 2:   If today were my last day, I would regret . . .

Chapter 3:   Am I in the right job, career and organization? If not, why?

Chapter 4:   What was I most fascinated with as a child?

Chapter 5:   Have I missed any critical road signs or clues about the direction I was traveling in life?

If so, why did I miss them?

Chapter 6:   What is my definition of success?

Chapter 7:   What am I most passionate about?

Chapter 8:   What do I want to be remembered for in life? Can I see that goal?

ANALYZE YOUR PRESENT SITUATION

Chapter 9: How accurately does my resume reflect what I am most passionate about?

How can I reflect this even stronger?

Chapter 10: What do I need to Subtract from my life?

What do I need to do Less of?

What do I need to Add to my life?

What do I need to do More of?

IMPROVING YOUR JOB AND CAREER

Chapter 16: What specific things can I do today to add more value to those around me?

Chapter 17: How does my purpose support the purpose of my organization? If it does not, how can I create this alignment in my life?

Chapter 18: What would I miss, if I left my current organization? Can these things be replaced elsewhere?

Chapter 19: How can I combine all that I love to do and make the money I need and want doing it?

Chapter 20: List all the jobs you worked in your life. Place an asterisk by the jobs you enjoyed most. Of the ones you asterisked force-rank the jobs from most-liked to least-liked.

Next make a list of the jobs you always wanted to try, but haven't had the courage or opportunity to attempt. Next to each of these jobs explain why you have not tried them then what is stopping you from attempting them now.

Now force-rank the list of jobs you wanted to try from most interesting to least interesting.

Chapter 21: WHY does my organization exist?

How does my job support my organization's WHY?

How does my WHY support my job's WHY?

Chapter 22: Are there important clues I am ignoring in life? If so, why and what are they?

Chapter 23: When in my life have I been so passionately focused on an activity that I lost track of time and what was I doing?

Chapter 24: What excuses am I making about not being able to have a job, career and life I love?

Chapter 25: Who else is successfully doing what I want to be doing and what is their strategy?

TAKING THE FIRST STEP

Chapter 26: What job would I be excited to share with others?

What kind of organizational purpose would inspire me to share it with others?

What gets me out of bed in the morning?

If I didn't need money, what would I do in life?

What do I do best?

What am I most passionate about?

What am I most interested in?

What have I most enjoyed doing throughout my life and why?

Chapter 27: What am I most focused on and is my focus in the right place?

Chapter 28: How can I be more present in my life?

SUPPLEMENTAL PURPOSE QUESTIONS

Throughout the course of this book I asked you to examine your life and career by answering questions with the intention of propelling you towards a job, career and life that you love. Use the questions in this section as additional tools to help with that end goal. Your answers will help guide you along your path using your Purpose M.A.P.™.

Human minds use intuitive and logical thoughts to process information in the two hemispheres of our brain, but both sides work seamlessly together. How each of us approaches a topic and conversation is equally diverse, but ultimately to achieve a successful conversation – even in our heads – we must listen to the question, examine it, absorb it then answer truthfully without fear, keeping everything in balance.

This book is about you and your future. Scary stuff to consider, but not so much when you realize that your future can be molded to achieve your dreams and your purpose. With this book you can do just that.

I've grouped the purpose-related questions in the following pages into categories, which I hope will allow your thoughts to focus on specific themes and promote 360 degree thinking similar to Edward de Bono's *Six Thinking Hats*.

<u>Foundation</u> **Purpose Questions** - your purpose baseline

<u>Heart</u> **Purpose Questions** - your emotions and feelings

<u>Mind</u> **Purpose Questions** - your engaged mind

<u>Fact</u> **Purpose Questions** - the facts you will need to consider

<u>Barrier</u> **Purpose Questions** - the things that could go wrong

<u>Opportunity</u> **Purpose Questions** - what will go right

<u>Alternative</u> **Purpose Questions** - other available options

Please answer each question honestly and thoughtfully. Remember there is no time limit so allow yourself to dwell on and sleep on your answers, as needed. If you don't know the answer right away, come back to it later.

FOUNDATION PURPOSE QUESTIONS

Your purpose baseline

Am I happy?

Am I fulfilled?

Am I living my purpose in life?

Am I doing what I do best?

Do I know what I do best?

Am I great at my job?

Do I like my job?

Do I love my job?

Am I disengaged in my job?

Am I sought after in my chosen career?

Do I like my career?

Do I love my career?

Am I disengaged in my career?

Do I like my current employer?

Do I love my current employer?

Am I disengaged at my current organization?

HEART PURPOSE QUESTIONS

Your emotions and feelings

Do I feel I am contributing to something important in life?

What are my biggest fears in life?

How do I make myself feel good?

How soon would I like to make a change to my job, career and life?

How does my current job make me feel?

How does my current career make me feel?

How does my current employer make me feel?

How do the people at my current organization make me feel?

How does my current boss make me feel?

How do I feel when I wake up on a workday?

How do I feel about changing jobs?

How do I feel about changing careers?

How do I feel about changing organizations?

How would doing what I love make me feel?

Do I feel well placed in my job?

Do I feel well placed in my career?

What great things am I currently doing in life?

How do I feel when talking about my job with family?

How do I feel when talking about my job with friends?

If I discover ways to get better at my current job and add more value with my work will I be happier and more engaged in it?

If I become a leading expert in my current career will I be happier and more engaged with it?

If I learn more about my current organization and its mission and purpose will I be happier and more engaged working there?

If I get to know my boss better will I perhaps like him/her more?

If I get to know my co-workers better will I perhaps like them more?

Could I be happier and more fulfilled in life?

What do I ultimately want in life?

What do I want to leave the world with?

Am I representing myself in the way I most want to be seen?

Am I proud of the accomplishments on my resume?

What types of cultures do I like most?

What have I liked most about the organizations I have worked for in the past?

What have I liked least about the organizations I have worked for in the past?

Am I adding value to others?

Am I present now?

Am I going to something or running away from something? In either case, why?

Do I live for weekends and vacations?

Can I easily distinguish my work and my play?

Would my definition of success be different if those close to me were more accepting of what I wanted to do?

How was and is my definition of success influenced by others?

Do I believe in what I am doing?

Do I love what I do?

Who will be waiting on the other side of my door to purpose?

Do I dress in a manner that makes me feel good about myself?

Who have I been kind to today?

Who will I be kinder to tomorrow?

Am I using the gifts I have been given?

MIND PURPOSE QUESTIONS

Your engaged mind

What decisions and commitments could I make now about my health and psychological outlook?

In what specific ways will I fulfill my purpose?

What did I spend most of my time doing in my youth?

What did I love most as a child?

Do I know and understand my organization's mission and purpose?

If I don't feel connected to the mission and purpose of my organization, have I spoken to my boss or someone else who can help?

Am I being distracted by "hard work" in life?

If I were to change my definition of success today, what would it be?

What is stopping me from changing my definition of success?

Do I know my natural talents? If so, what are they?

Am I actively and proactively exercising and developing my talents into strengths?

Is my organization, a mentor, or someone else helping me develop my talents into strengths?

How can I position myself in life to take better advantage of my natural talents and developed strengths and do what I am most passionate about?

How can I get to a place in life where I am doing what I am best at and love at least 80% of the time? What is my plan? Are there people I can ask to assist me in achieving this plan? Who can I ask to mentor me that might be already living my plan?

Could I afford to take a reduction in pay to do a job I enjoyed more?

What is stopping me from making a change in life? What can I do to lift these barriers and mitigate my risks?

Am I keeping my eyes open for clues as to what I should be doing in life?

Am I in tune with my emotions about my job, career and life?

Am I taking the time to ask myself questions, answering honestly and listening to my responses?

What advice would I give to my younger self about my choices in life?

Are there things I can do without to provide me the opportunity to live a purpose-driven and happier life?

What did I learn from times in my life in which I had to let go of something I loved?

What are the opportunities I am missing by spending time focusing on excuses?

How can I revise my strategy to start winning?

Who can help me with my strategy and perhaps shed a new light on my challenges and opportunities?

Who and what are causing me to doubt myself and are there valid concerns?

Do I feel confident with where my focus is and if not, why?

Am I as fit as I could be?

If not, what achievable, small goals can improve my health?

Am I focusing on the negative or positive experiences in my life?

Who are the five people I spend most of my time with and how do they impact my life? (List them)

FACT PURPOSE QUESTIONS

The facts you will need to consider

What is making me happy in life and why?

What is making me unhappy in life and why?

Do I love my job, career and life? If not, why?

What is most important to me in life?

How much money do I need to live comfortably?

What things in life can I do without (e.g., car, memberships, subscriptions, large home)?

What factors do I need to consider before making a job, career and life change (e.g., income, bonuses, stock vesting, time in my current role, not having medical benefits or the high cost of potentially getting them)?

What is making me feel fulfilled in life?

What is making me feel unfulfilled in life?

Why do I like my job?

Why do I love my job?

Why am I disengaged in my job?

Why do I like my career?

Why do I love my career?

Why am I disengaged in my career?

Why do I like my current employer?

Why do I love my current employer?

Why am I disengaged at my organization?

What is my annual income?

What benefits do I now have to consider?

What are my annual expenses?

How much savings do I have?

What is the realistic value of my sellable belongs?

Where would I most like to live?

Do I have a partner? Children? If so, where would they like to live?

What other career options do I currently have?

What other income options do I currently have?

What contacts do I have to help me make a job or career change?

Do I have a mentor?

Who else can I reach out to for help (people/organizations)?

What tools and resources are available to assist me in a new job/ career search (e.g., Monster.com, recruiters, assessments like Clifton StrengthsFinder®)?

How soon can I make a change to my job, career and life?

How long can I support myself and family without income?

Do I have childcare issues to consider?

What important contributions am I making to my community?

What important contributions am I making to the world?

Am I healthy?

Do I feel good?

Do I have the discipline to work for myself?

What is my level of education?

What experience do I have to rely on?

What do other people say I do best?

BARRIER PURPOSE QUESTIONS

The things that could go wrong

What are the risks if I leave my job or change my career?

What could go wrong if I make a major change in my life now?

How could my decision to make a change negatively impact my partner and/or family?

Can I go back to my old job/employer if things don't work out?

What personal sacrifices am I going to have to make to follow a new path?

What sacrifices will my family have to make if I follow a new path? Are they willing to make these sacrifices? Do they have a choice?

How is my health and psychological outlook on life being negatively impacted by the job, career and life decisions I am making?

Who are the people that work against me in life (List them)?

Can I tell them how they make me feel or interact with them less or not at all?

What are the risks if I leave my job?

What negative reactions will I get from others to a job change?

What negative reactions will I get from others to a career change?

What negative reactions will I get from others to a life change?

How will I be worse off moving to a new job?

How will I be worse off moving to a new career?

How will I be worse off moving to a new organization?

What happens if the grass isn't greener on the other side?

How will my level of education hold me back?

What has gone wrong with others trying to make a job change?

What has gone wrong with others trying to make a career change?

What has gone wrong with others trying to make an employer change?

What has gone wrong with others trying to make a life change?

What if I don't have the discipline to work for myself?

OPPORTUNITY PURPOSE QUESTIONS

What will go right

What will be the benefits of a job or career change for me and my family?

What are some job and career-change success stories?

What is my best-case job or career-change scenario?

What will my life look like after success?

Who are the people that will be my biggest supporters of a job, career and life change (List them)?

How can I do something I love and make the money I need and want doing it?

How can I make my family and myself happy at the same time?

How can I have more fun?

How will my educational level help me?

What are all my current job opportunities (List them)?

What are all my current career opportunities (List them)?

What are all my current life opportunities (List them)?

ALTERNATIVE PURPOSE QUESTIONS

Other available options

What could I do on the side without quitting my job that would give me the fulfillment I am looking for? What is stopping me from doing it?

What other options do I have in life that would make me happy?

What is stopping me from pursuing them?

Do I have to change my job, career and life to find happiness? If so, why and what changes are needed? Am I prepared to commit to these changes?

Can I start my own business or buy one that already exists (or a franchise)? If so, what type?

Do I have the self-discipline to work for myself?

What other viable alternatives do I have to make my life better?

Can I commit to these alternatives?

Can I afford and feel comfortable not earning income for a period of time during my transition? If so, how long?

Could I go back to school part or full-time to learn something new? If so, what, where could I go and when could I start?

What other creative actions or moves can I make in my life to set me on the right path?

What other jobs can I interview for?

Can I get funding to support what I want to do most?

Can I get others to help me run a business while I do something else to generate the income I need?

Can I afford never to earn money again?

OBSERVATION QUESTIONS

(pre-interview) from:

"How to Find a Job, Career and Life You Love" by Louis Efron

Copy or download this page at LouisEfron.com for each potential employer, then answer the questions.

ORGANIZATION NAME: _____

JOB TITLE: _____

I. WEBSITE

☐ Visit the 'About Us' section of the company website. Study the company history, read any Executive bios and note if the company highlights aspects about their culture.

☐ Read company press releases or other posted news items. *You can also do a simple Google search to find news articles or postings regarding the company.*

☐ Locate articles describing company culture. *Sometimes these links are found on the career page.*

o Does the company culture fit my needs?

o   Make a note regarding their type of culture and keep that in mind when you go for an interview.

☐   Notes after reviewing Annual Report on investor relations page:

2. **JOB DESCRIPTION**

☐   Does the job description include requirements like "must have flexible hours" or be a "self-starter with limited guidance"? If so, do these fit with my life and work style?

☐   Do they describe the culture by including phrases like "fun environment", "employee should have a sense of humor" or "casual Fridays"? Or is it all business? Which appeals to me?

☐   Do they require certifications or college degrees or do they also allow for equivalent work experience?

☐ Are there misspellings or confusing language?

3. WORK LOCATION

☐ Do I like the community/area where the job is located?

☐ What is the cost of living in the area (taxes, house prices/rents)?

☐ How far will I need to commute to work and places I enjoy and how convenient will it be?

☐ What are the schools like?

☐ How far will I be from family and friends?

☐ Will I like the weather where I will need to live?

☐ Does the area support the things I like to do in life? *For example, walk, run, bike, hike, ski, dine out, visit museums, see film and live theatre.*

4. WORKING HOURS

☐ If accessible, how early/late do I see cars in the organization's parking lot? *Remember to take into consideration possible night shifts.*

5. TIME OFF

☐ Will the organization value and support what I value most in life?

☐ Will this job/organization allow me the time to focus on what is most important to me in life?

6. DRESS CODE

☐ What were employees wearing when I visited the organization?

☐ Is this the usual attire or was I visiting on a casual Friday?

☐ Am I comfortable with the organization's work attire?

7. RECEPTIONIST INTERACTION

☐ Is the receptionist friendly and inviting?

☐ Was I placed on hold indefinitely?

☐ Was I serviced in a timely and efficient manner? Or did my calls frequently get disconnected or routed improperly?

8. CLEANLINESS

☐ Is the exterior of the building clean? What about the parking lots?

9. AVAILABILITY

☐ How long did it take to schedule interviews for me?

☐ Did my interview get rescheduled more than once?

10. CARE

☐ Is the company involved in their surrounding community?

☐ Do they sponsor any charities or non-profit groups?

11. ACKNOWLEDGEMENT (OF YOU OR OTHERS)

☐ Do they treat their potential employees with care or do they rush off the phone after scheduling an interview or answering a question?

12. VISUAL CLUES

☐ What did I learn about the mission, purpose and values of the organization based on an exterior view of the job site?

INTERVIEW QUESTIONS

from

"How to Find a Job, Career and Life You Love" by Louis Efron

ORGANIZATION NAME: _____

JOB TITLE: _____

I. WORK LOCATION

Questions to ask your potential employer:

☐ Will I be required to work in the office or is there a remote working option? *If you don't like being stuck in an office five days a week, don't take a job at an organization that requires this.*

☐ How flexible and results-oriented is the organization's culture? *You will find the greatest flexibility in Results-Only Work Environments. I have included a website in Additional Resources for more information about these organizations.*

☐ What do employees like most about living in [insert job area]?

☐ Where do most employees live?

2. WORKING HOURS

Question to ask your potential employer:

☐ What hours do employees of [insert organization name] traditionally work?

3. **TIME OFF**

Question to ask your potential employer:

☐ One thing(s) that is very important to me in life is _____. How does [insert organization name] support such interests?

4. **DRESS CODE**

These items are internal questions for <u>you</u> to answer:

☐ What were employees wearing when I visited the organization?

☐ Is this the usual attire or was I visiting on a casual Friday?

☐ Am I comfortable with the organization's work attire?

Question to ask your potential employer:

☐   What is the dress code at [insert organization name]?

5.   **RECEPTIONIST INTERACTION**

These items are internal questions for <u>you</u> to answer:

☐   Was the receptionist friendly and inviting?

☐   Did the receptionist interact with others passing their work area?

6.   **CLEANLINESS**

These items are internal questions for <u>you</u> to answer:

☐   What does the lobby look like? Hallways? Offices? Are things clean and well-kept or dirty and unorganized?

☐ Is this the type of working environment that will make me comfortable?

7. **AVAILABILITY**

These items are internal questions for <u>you</u> to answer:

☐ How long did it take to schedule interviews for me?

☐ Did my interview get rescheduled more than once?

Questions to ask your potential employer:

☐ [To your potential manager] How much access will I have to you for assistance, coaching and mentoring?

☐ [To your potential manager] How much interaction do you like to have with your employees? *This question is helpful to ask if you prefer to work closely with your manager or more independently.*

8. CARE

These items are internal questions for <u>you</u> to answer:

☐ Is the company involved in their surrounding community?

☐ Do they sponsor any charities or non-profit groups?

☐ Did I have to wait in the lobby well past my scheduled interview time? If so, did anyone apologize or explain the reason why?

☐ Did my interviewers ask thoughtful questions and let me speak and fully answer what they asked?

☐ Did my interviewers seem present with me or distracted by others, incoming emails or phone calls?

☐ Were my interviewers prepared for my interview and had they reviewed my resume?

☐ Was there anything I saw while visiting the organization that would indicate a lack of care for employees? *For example, unclean restrooms, dirty hallways, smoking allowed in front of all entry doors, poor lighting or working conditions.*

Questions to ask your potential employer:

- [ ] What types of employee engagement programs does [insert organization name] have?

- [ ] How do employees usually characterize (or describe) the culture at [insert organization name]?

9. ACKNOWLEDGEMENT (OF YOU OR OTHERS)

These items are internal questions for _you_ to answer:

- [ ] While I was waiting for my interview, did people at the reception desk or in the lobby or hallways acknowledge or interact with me? Were they positive interactions?

- [ ] Did anyone acknowledge me when I walked through the halls to get to my meetings?

Questions to ask your potential employer:

☐ What is the employee culture like at [insert organization name]?

☐ How are employees recognized at [insert organization name]?

10. **VISUAL CLUES**

These items are internal questions for <u>you</u> to answer:

☐ What did I learn about the mission, purpose and values of the organization?

☐ How much can I tell about the organization's culture, mission, purpose and values from being at their location?

☐ Does the organization appear to live its values? *For example, if caring for employees is an organizational value, does the organization have an employee gym, recreation area, meditation rooms, on-site child care and new mother facilities, subsidized meals, generous time off policy, free cereal bar or a dream room?*

☐ Do employees at all levels call each other by their first names or address each other formally?

☐ Do employees eat lunch together or at their desks alone?

☐ Is the organization's culture a culture I am comfortable with and interested in?

Questions to ask your potential employer:

- [ ] What are the mission, purpose and values of [insert organization name]? *Check the organization's website before your interview to determine if this question is needed. Or rephrase the question to suit, if questions arise after reviewing their website.*

- [ ] What is most important to the people who work at [insert organization name]?

- [ ] [To your potential manager] What is most important to you as a manager (or leader) at [insert organization name]?

AFTER THE INTERVIEW IS OVER . . .

☐ Based on all the information I have, am I passionate
about working for this organization and will I fit into
the culture?

Purpose Master Action Plan™ Template

(Available as a download at LouisEfron.com)

PURPOSE M.A.P.™	
NAME:	DATE:
QUESTIONS	ANSWERS
1. What is my current Purpose Alignment Indicator Score™?	
2. What is my definitive statement about the difference I am trying to make in the world – my purpose (Chapter 33)?	
3. What is the worthy ideal I am trying to achieve (Chapter 34)?	
4. What is the description of the person I have decided to become (Chapter 34)?	
5. What is my 30-Day goal(s) to support my purpose, worthy ideal and me (Make this S.M.A.R.T.)?	
6. What is my 30-Day action(s) to achieve my goal(s)?	
7. What is my 30-Day outcome(s)?	
8. What is my new Purpose Alignment Indicator Score™?	
9. Has my Purpose Alignment Indicator Score™ changed for the better or worse?	
10. What do I need to action on my next 30-Day Purpose M.A.P.™ to improve my purpose alignment?	
Create a new 30-Day Purpose M.A.P.™ now	

ADDITIONAL RESOURCES

If you are having problems answering/rating any of the questions/statements in this book or need additional assistance finding and following your purpose in life, below are a few resources to help.

If you are in need of further assistance or purpose coaching, please email me at Louis@LouisEfron.com.

Get a Life, Not a Job: Do What You Love and Let Your Talents Work For You by Dr. Paula Caligiuri has excellent personal discovery exercises throughout.

The Pathfinder: How to Choose or Change Your Career for a Lifetime of Satisfaction and Success by Nicholas Lore is a helpful comprehensive workbook of career discovery.

Aspire by Kevin Hall is a wonderfully inspiring book about purpose.

The Tao of Pooh by Benjamin Hoff is a classic, simple, fun and impactful story about finding your path within. I read it once a year.

Six Thinking Hats – the international bestseller by Edward de Bono.

Now, Discover Your Strengths by Marcus Buckingham and Donald O. Clifton will help you better understand what you do best.

LouisEfron.com – My Purpose Alignment Indicator Survey™ and other resources.

Clifton StrengthsFinder® (gallupstrengthscenter.com) tool will profile your strengths.

Y Scouts (yscouts.com) – A Purpose Based Executive Search Firm.

GameChangers 500 (gamechangers500.com) – The world's top purpose-driven organizations and the people behind them.

CultureRx (gorowe.com) – More information about Results-Only Work Environments (ROWE) and companies that embrace the principle.

The Purpose Institute (thepurposeinstitute.com) and Bright-House (thinkbrighthouse.com) - offers services to organizations looking to discover and bring to life their purpose. The sites are a good source for employees, managers and leaders looking to understand how purpose works in an organization.

Steve Jobs' 2005 Stanford Commencement Speech – speech on purpose. Inspirational!

Your Body Language Shapes Who You Are – Amy Cuddy's amazing video on generating confidence.

Why You Will Fail to Have a Great Career – Larry Smith's insightful and humorous video on barriers to career happiness.

A Life of Purpose – Rich Warren's inspiring and enlightening video.

Brendon Burchard's Total Product Blueprint and Experts Academy (BrendonBurchard.com), both extremely valuable for all those interested in running their own business and furthering their personal development.

Elance.com – Freelance designers, programmers, developers, writers and marketers from around the world at your fingertips at a budget you can afford.

Kickstarter.com – No strings attached investor crowd-funding. A very cool concept and relatively easy to start!

BEHIND THE
SCENES

ABOUT ME, THE AUTHOR

This book is full of questions about YOU. So here is a little about ME: Louis Efron!

- I spent eight years in the arts as a director, manager and producer on Broadway, Off-Broadway and Off-Off-Broadway before shifting to a career in corporate America.

- I worked eleven years for the Fortune 300 Medical Device company, Stryker, working on four continents while living in three: North America, Europe, Asia and Africa.

- For two years I worked in the IT industry as VP of international human resources for a mid-sized firm.

- I am the founder of Louis Efron, LLC – The Voice of Purpose – assisting individuals and organizations in discovering and living their purpose, achieving fulfillment and success.

- I won my first writing accolade at the age ten: second place in a Phoenix, Arizona school district-wide creative writing contest for a short story entitled *The Five Headed Giant vs. The Three Headed Deadly Snake*.

- I am currently a writer, speaker, coach, trainer, teacher, consultant, film producer and director, husband, father and humanitarian. My work has been seen by millions around the world and my articles on Forbes.com have hit #1 on *Forbes*, Twitter, and LinkedIn.

- I am an advisor to Y Scouts, a purpose-based executive search firm in Tempe, AZ.

- In 2012, I founded World Child Cancer USA to save the lives of children around the world with treatable cancer. Like so many others, my life has been personally touched by the horrors of cancer. I lost my sixty-nine year old father to the disease just two weeks before the birth of my first daughter and watched other family members and friends battle with the terrible illness, too.

- In 2014, I turned my attention to another important cause near and dear to my heart – education – and my partnership with Pencils of Promise in an effort to raise money to build schools for children in developing countries.

- I studied Labor Relations at Cornell University, New York State School of Industrial and Labor Relations and Advanced Leadership at Harvard Business School. I hold a BA from

California State University, Fullerton, plus a BS and JD from Saratoga University School of Law.

- I am also a certified StrengthsFinder® coach helping people discover what they do best.

- I am blessed with a loving wife and two beautiful daughters.

Contact Details for Louis Efron:

Louis Efron, LLC

LouisEfron.com

Louis@LouisEfron.com

ACKNOWLEDGEMENTS

Special thanks to:

My gorgeous and talented wife and the first reader of everything I write, Evie, for putting up with my late nights and mission to change the world. I was blessed the day I moved to England and met you. I love you.

My two beautiful daughters, Anya Rose and Ella Brae, who remind me every day what unconditional love is and how magical an un-inhibited mind can be.

My father, who taught me to look for the positives in everything and that anything is possible in life. You were my biggest fan. I miss and think about you every day.

My mother, who made every day of my childhood a day in Disney-land and continues to do so. I love you dearly and I am eternally grateful for the life you have given me and how much you have always cared.

My grandfathers, who taught me the power of perseverance and my grandmothers, who taught me what love and strength are about.

My brother Danny, sisters Elizabeth, Tammy, Shoshana and Jenny, brother-in-laws, sister-in-law, nieces, nephew, parents-in-law, and friends who make my life complete and always fun.

Nathan Means, my extraordinary editor, thought partner and friend. You have made me a better writer and gave me the confidence I needed to stay the course and write this book.

Barbara A. Bagwell, my second edition editor and dear friend since college. Thank you for pushing me and inspiring me to make this second edition even more helpful to my readers, further fulfilling my purpose.

Peter Jones, for his impressive book design and support.

Dan Gerstein, for kicking off my professional writing career with an introduction to his *Forbes* editor.

Fred Allen, my *Forbes* editor, who believed I could add value to his prestigious magazine.

Eric Nelson, my agent, for always being available for feedback and guidance on my career path as a writer.

Don Stafford, my first real boss, who taught me about responsibility and being kind to others.

Dean Hess, my theatrical directing mentor and dear friend, who opened my eyes to the magic of great theatre and exemplifies for me what loving life is all about.

Mike Tzaneteas, my first corporate boss and dear friend, who taught me everything I needed to know about human resources and caring for the people of an organization.

Lisa Peterson, my guardian angel, mentor and dear friend. Your guidance, coaching, honesty, friendship, love and trust have been defining factors in my career success.

Brian Mohr, for opening the door into the Arizona purpose community, your numerous and kind introductions and your friendship. Our paths were joined for a reason.

Howard Getson, for being unexpected help when I needed it most.

Kevin Hall, for his wonderful foreword, support, guidance and friendship.

Chester Elton, Ann Rhoades, Ruth Ross, Linda Scull, Pat Beyer, Greg Jordan, John Schaefer, Max Hansen, Mark Christensen and Chris Smith for their kind words, assistance and support.

NOTES

NOTES

NOTES

NOTES

NOTES

CPSIA information can be obtained
at www.ICGtesting.com
Printed in the USA
LVOW13s0915230718
584633LV00004B/492/P